DENOMINATIONAL STEW: AMERICAN STYLE
A CHRISTIAN STUDY GUIDE

Dr. Lyndel M. Stephenson

WESTBOW°
PRESS
A DIVISION OF THOMAS NELSON
& ZONDERVAN

WestBow Press books may be ordered through booksellers or by contacting:

WestBow Press
A Division of Thomas Nelson & Zondervan
1663 Liberty Drive
Bloomington, IN 47403
www.westbowpress.com
1 (866) 928-1240

ISBN: 978-1-4908-3380-4 (sc)

Library of Congress Control Number: 2014906900

Printed in the United States of America.

WestBow Press rev. date: 05/28/2014

Understanding Christian Denominations in America today.

Who are they?

What are they about?

How did it all happen?

Which is the right one for you?

Acknowledgments

This book is dedicated to my brother, Larry E. Stephenson Sr.

and his devoted wife, Carol. Without their dedication to

God and family this work would never have survived.

A special thanks to my Mentor and my friend, Chaplain Carfrey of Keen, Texas, whose love and kindness helped me through some pretty rough times. I want to thank Katie, John, Stephanie, and all the good people at Office Depot in Baytown, and Houston, Texas, not only for their generosity and professionalism, but also for being all around good people. Timothy Lopez of the El Paso Library for helping me walk through the maze of computer technology. Lastly, my sincere gratitude goes out to Doctor Rice of Shalom Bible College & Seminary, for her encouragement, instruction, and true devotion to the Christian walk.

Just Because A Thousand People
Tell The Same Lie,
It Doesn't Make a Lie the Truth.

Forward

Denominational Stew is written in a manner that reminds me of Revelation 10 "…sweet as honey to the palate yet bitter to the stomach [paraphrasing]." Having begun in apologetics, dealing with the varied denominations/cults mentioned in Dr. Stephenson's book, the pages are full of a refreshing reminder of the battle we are faced with as Christians. A refreshing reminder of our roots as well. Keeping it simple, Dr. Stephenson has penned his thoughts in a unique caption called *"Denominational Stew; American Style."* All are called to make a defense of what we believe, being ready in and out of season (I Peter 3:15 & II Timothy 4:1-3). We can appreciate the historical and present the truth of our journey.

Not written as a summary of the Bible, but rather as a summary of American Christianity itself, this book emphasizes the negatives as well as the positives of American denominationalism. Some will read his book and challenge the writer rather than the points being presented. What a shame! After reading *Denominational Stew* the first time, I set it down for a few days then reread it again. After this 2nd reading, I gained a better appreciation of the presentation of his thoughts. During first readings, I generally read to see what I'll learn. The 2nd reading, I'll try to read it in the spirit in which it was written. This way I can sense whether the Spirit of God has inspired the writer or not. This book, being refreshing, honors our Lord with an abundance of facts and Truth.

I read volumes of books every year and find many are full of skewed views where I have to have my "discernment hat" on. Not so with this book! It has been an honor to read and to reread this book for shear enjoyment.

Chaplain Don Downie

Contents

Introduction

As many will testify to, I was not a very good person. I was exactly the "type" Paul wrote about in Romans 1 and Galatians 5:19-21. Then on Fathers Day of 2003 the healing power of God stepped into my life and I was changed---recreated---transformed into a new creature. Yes, I had met Jesus and accepted Him as my *Lord and Savior.* That same day I was baptized in the prison Chapel. On Father's Day I had received a new Father! Now how cool is that!

But along with a new heart, a new purpose, and the indwelling of the Holy Spirit, I also acquired a new problem. See, I was to be released soon, and as a New Believer I had no idea which church to attend. There are hundreds of denominations to choose from and thousands of churches with snappy titles to check out. But which one is the right one for me? I'm sure this question also plagues many other Believers; both new as well as old alike. Of course, there's a difference between the *Spiritual Church* (the collective body of Believers, often called "the Bride") and the *Earthly Church* (organizations of Believers who meet in a physical building to fellowship and to worship together). Scripture does command us to attend church and to be a part of the fellowship: "Not forsaking the assembling of ourselves together" (Hebrews 10:25).

All of the seemingly endless listings of churches and denominations in phone books and newspapers only enhance one's confusion. Where did they all come from? Surely, they "all" can't be the "one" designed by the Father, established by the Son, and empowered by the Holy Ghost! How did it all happen? How did the Church of the Father, Son, and Holy Ghost mutate into all these denominations: Baptist, Catholic, Episcopal, Quakers, Methodist, Mennonites, Pentecostals and all the others? In addition, don't forget those islands unto themselves, the so-called "Non-Denominationals."

America, with all its rich history and its grand mix of cultures has been called "the Melting Pot." America's Christian structure can also be seen in the same light, except I see it more as a big pot of chunky stew. Not a salad that just sits there. Our Christian Stew is dynamic, boiling, rolling, ever changing and continually receiving new ingredients. Parts of this *Stew* have blended together to give it it's uniquely American flavor, yet one can still distinguish its various parts: a slice of doctorial carrot; an imported potato; a piece of cultural celery or hunk of traditional meat. All this is continually rolling and mixing together to form our great *Denominational Stew; American Style.*

But is it all healthy? Which parts should we eat? Is it more American ideals than scriptural ideals? Are all of its ingredients directed by God or are they man-directed? These are important questions all Believers need to investigate. The following book was born out of this need: the need to sort out today's Christian Denominations and to discover the truth God established for His worship.

Enjoy…

Dr. Lyndel M. Stephenson

PART ONE
The Roots of Change

I.

<u>FREEDOM TO CHANGE</u>

America---the New World---Land of Liberty---U.S.A.---or the Melting Pot. By whatever name one refers to this amazing country, one thing is certain: it's synonymous with "change." There has never been a collective nation of such inventors, entrepreneurs, free thinkers and capable people as Americans. We change things; develop ideas; nurture concepts and solve problems…and always in a big, big way. In world changing ways!

There's something in the American attitude that fosters change. We change jobs, cars, philosophies, pets and spouses with great ease. Rather than the eagle as our national icon, we should adopt the TV remote control as our symbol. A symbol of change. Very little goes unchanged in this New World of ours and this includes Christianity. It has changed a lot…

Of course, Christianity didn't originate in the U.S.A. It came to this Melting Pot, this *Stew Pot,* in the sails of the Mayflower. It was in the ideologies of brave settlers, in the hearts of the colonist, in the dreams of speculators and in the hopes of every Puritan seeking a better life. Seeking a changed life. Each brought and planted in fertile soil his or her own personal seed of ideas. Individuality flourished: personal freedom meant the freedom to worship God in one's own way without being forced to worship in the State approved way. Freedom of religion was a "right" endorsed by God Himself! That's what our country was built on.

FIRST AMENDMENT

This "right" to the free exercise of one's religion was so important to our Founding Fathers that it became our First Amendment to the *United States Constitution* (ratified in 1791).

> "Congress shall make no law respecting an establishment of religion or prohibiting the free exercise thereof." (Rhodes 13)

The Colonial freedom of religion slashed through the cords of tradition and conformity. In this *E Pluribus Unum,* America's kettle of Christianity covered the whole spectrum of worship. Resulting in everything from the modest one-room country church to the fast-talking celebrity televangelist with worldwide podiums. We have it all: speaking in tongues; baptism by immersion or by sprinkling; musical instruments allowed or not allowed; men preachers, women preachers, Old Testament, New Testament or just the *Sermon On The Mount*. We have small churches; mega churches; the Lord's Supper; fasting; and any of the dozens of *Bible* translations on the market in almost any language you like. No longer is Christianity a simple soup…it has become a rich, full fledged, Chunky *Stew*.

Yes, Christianity today is radically different from the one founded along the barren roads of Judea by Jesus and the twelve. Somehow, the image of a loving Jesus wearing a white robe and dusty sandals while humbly proclaiming the Kingdom of God, has changed into high profile super-preachers (some of them women) wearing thousand dollar suits while screaming into high tech sound systems proclaiming "partnerships for donations!"

This evolution---this change---from simple first century worship to modern American Christianity is highlighted with bold leaders, powerful movements, fallen martyrs and an unshakable faith in change. That is, "faith" that God will guide change in the right direction. In the direction of His Kingdom. That He would do for us as He did for the ancient Israelites at the foot of Mt Sinai and "show us how He wants to be worshiped." But of course, each denomination believes "it" is the receiver of that way.

Today there are approximately 1,200 different Christian denominations or movements in America, and none of them stands alone. Each came from a previous denomination or movement. Moving from one belief system to another, they are all related by the very forces that changed them into what they are now. Forces such as politics, innovative theological views, scriptural interpretations, and the search for truth---search for money---freedom of speech---and even science and new historical revelations. To understand how this happened and how denominationalism grew so rapidly is to pick at our history and look at the ingredients of this great *American Stew of Denominationalism.*

II.

<u>WHAT'S IN A WORD</u>

The place to begin our understanding of this Melting Pot of ideas is with the word itself. The English word "denomination" comes from the Latin word *"denominare,"* which means "to name." A denomination can be defined as "the name of an association **within a religion** that shows and shares the same beliefs, practices, and cooperates with each other to develop and maintain unity" (Rhodes 12).

This idea of grouping together based on shared beliefs is nothing new. We are social animals (so to speak) and seek out like-minded companions. Sects, orders, clubs, clicks, and even gangs are to some extent synonymous with denominations. Even the name "Christian" is noteworthy because the early followers of Jesus-the-Christ were recognized as a sect or separate group. Although they "came out" of Judaism they were distinct from it and as well as from all other sects of the ancient world (Rhodes 7).

As previously stated, "no denomination stands alone." Each came from something before it. Jesus, the originator of Christianity (although it was called "the Way" at the time) was born a Jew and raised in the religion of the Jews: "Judaism." Jesus had stepped out of the family tradition (on His mother's side anyway) and presented the world something new. He built on Judaism and took it to the next level. It was no longer a denomination of <u>waiting</u> for the Messiah, but one of the <u>arrival</u> of the Messiah. Like Jesus said in Matthew 5:17 "…I am not come to destroy the law, but to fulfill."

Jesus was a Jew by birth: an Israelite by heritage and raised in Galilee. It is a fundamental error, but a common one today, to use the words "Jew" and "Israelite" interchangeably. Understanding this difference is essential to understanding the *Stew*. They are not a single ingredient but are two separate ingredients. An excerpt from the 1998 *Jewish Almanac, Part 1* titled *"Identity Crisis…History for the Term Jew,"* tells us "It is incorrect to call an ancient Israelite a Jew" (Peters 20).

An example of how easy it is to get these two names mixed up is found in Revelation 7:4, speaking of the 144,000 first fruits; "…all of the tribes of the children of Israel" (KJV). However, some careless speakers (for whatever the reason) teach it as "…of all the tribes of the Jews." An error. That is like calling all Americans "Texans" because Texas is a part of America. Just as all Jews "are" Israelites but not all Israelites are Jews. To teach "that it doesn't matter what you call a people," verges on a sin. It is the sin of teaching falsehood for truth. If we are not going to teach TRUTH then we may as well go back to paganism and call that truth too.

Because it is so important to understand the difference as well as the similarities of the ingredients of American Christian Denominations, we need to take a scenic side trip back to the basics. Back to the beginning. Back to the Garden.

III.

<u>THE GARDEN TO THE CROSS</u>

At creation, God made Adam and Woman. (Her name wasn't Eve until after the fall [see Geneses 2:23 & 3:20] then he called her Eve). They had no nationally or titled religion. If you were to ask Adam, "What is your religion?" He'd look at you confused, as if you were the world's first nut case! The first couple was simply "mankind" and worshipped God. The only God. The God of Creation. There was nothing else to them---not even the idea of anything else.

At creation, Adam rose from the clay worshipping God. It was natural. It was what he, and we, were designed to do! Made in the image of God, in the Holy image of the Godhead (Genesis 1:26). Adam worshipped God as easily and natural as the wind blows through the treetops…by God's design and wonder. Anything else is fake and brings chaos.

Enter Satan. Satan showed up and things changed! He instigated the domino effect of changes and denominations by getting Woman to consider a different interpretation of God's words. The Serpent quizzed her, "Did God really say you'd die?"(Genesis 3:4). This was the <u>first doctrinal issue in man's history</u>. Everything changed that day in the Garden. Doubt brought sin. Sin brought change. We're still doing it today. Changing… sinning… changing and sinning some more to make up for the changes…

With the first sin came the first punishment (Genesis 3:14-19), then the first forgiveness (3:21), and then the first orders to move (3:23-24). Kicked out of the Garden and told to get a real job; "In the sweat of thy face shalt thou eat…" (3:19). Our power of choice, the power to exercise our will, to make changes, had reared its first blow to worship. The desire for change had begun.

CAIN & ABEL

The first couple moved out of the Garden and started having babies. The next change came when their first-born son, Cain, killed his younger brother, Abel. This first murder was rooted in the second doctrinal issue; one over "offerings." Cain, like his Mother, had reinterpreted God's word and did it his own way. He offered grain instead of prime livestock. His brand new denomination of Grain Givers had resulted in murder. He had been rejected by God and felt angry. This was way before Anger Management classes were created so he made a change in religious practice and killed the one who had pleased God (Genesis 4:4-8). Killing the ones God is pleased with has become a tradition which mankind, for some reason, will choose to continue.

Cain's choices changed things drastically. He, like his parents before him, was told by God to move (4:16). As world population grew so did its desire to change the rules. This went on until God stepped in and changed the weather, which resulted in a worldwide flood (Genesis 6:5-7). He was washing the Kettle clean to start again.

After the flood mankind did the "be fruitful and multiply" thing again. As the population swelled, they built cities and came up with a new industry: that of tower building. The tower of Babel to be exact. Some men wanted to change the rules of "how to get to Heaven" (Genesis 11:4) so they built a tower to reach it. They wanted to build their tower tall enough so that they could climb up and walk right into God's front room: His throne room! This was the <u>next major step in new doctrine</u>: "getting to Heaven by works rather than by faith." Blending man's personal desires with theology and God's Word is a prideful undertaking. So God "confounded their language" (Genesis 11:9). Not only would different languages have a later effect on denominations (in *Bible* translations) but it also forced men to move again.

People banded together into groups based on a common language. This was actually the beginnings of nations: another new concept for mankind. Rules and traditions changed as nations grew. Eventually, in the same manner as the serpent "helped" Eve, mankind created new gods in his "own image." He gave worship to rock formations, planets, stars, charms, statues, and let his imagination pretty much do the thinking for him. If it feels good, worship it! He created many new gods, and with the devious help of Satan, devised complex ways of worship. If a person was not satisfied with his or her god or the rules of worship, they could switch (like changing channels) to another more sensual, fun religion. New nations---new languages---new gods---and new sects: no longer was it only a question of "how to worship," but one of "who to worship."

Just as Eve had decided to bend the rules a little to fit her own personal desires rather then God's desires (see Genesis 3:6), Satan now had the majority of the human race changing things based on their own personal desires. Rather than being based on God's word, these new religions and practices were rooted on the world and its desires:

> 15. "Love not the world, neither the things that are in the world. If any man love the world, the love of the Father is not in him."
>
> 16. "For all that is not the world, the lust of the flesh,

and the lust of the eyes, and the pride of life, is not of the Father but is of the world." (I John 2:15-16)

However, not all men had turned away from the One True God.

A group of people who held fast to worshipping God the Father were called (in ancient Hebrew) "Ya'ho'tas," meaning "followers of Yah, or God." They followed an oral tradition and could trace their ancestry back to Shem of the Ark and even back to Adam's third son, Seth. They would later be referred to as "Semites," from their root-ancestor, "Shem." This is where we get the term "anti-Semitic:" anyone who is against the ancestors of Shem.

ABRAM

One such Semite named Abram would father the entire nation, which would eventually come to be known as "Hebrews." Abram, from the city of Ur, was called by God to "pack up and leave home." He settled in an area called "Hebron" and God was very pleased with him. So pleased that he made a covenant with Abram; changed his name to Abraham; and told him "to move:"

> 1. "Now the LORD had said unto Abram, Get thee out of thy country…unto the land that I will shew thee." (Genesis 12:1)

> 5. "Neither shall thy name any more be called Abram, but thy name shall be Abraham, for a father of many nations have I made out of thee." (Genesis 17:5)

Abram's son, Isaac, had a son, named Jacob. Jacob eventually had twelve sons (and a daughter). Then after an all-night, wrestling match, Jacob's name was changed to "Israel" (32:28). This made his twelve sons the "twelve sons of Israel," which later grew into the "Twelve Tribes of Israel:" the covenant people of God. They ended up enslaved in Egypt for 430 years (Exodus 1:11). This brings us to the next vital ingredient of the *Stew*: Moses the Lawgiver.

MOSES

At 80 years old, God sent the Hebrew, Moses, back to Egypt to rescue His People. God's chosen people. Moses did as commanded and led the nation of Israel out of Egypt and into the desert, right up to God's footstool: Mt. Sinai. There God gave the Israelites a complete set of His Laws. They were dictated by God and written down by Moses. These rules of conduct and worship became known as the "Mosaic Laws."

With the rules finally written down it would be very difficult to change any or to question them. However, of course, some would try. Under the leadership of Korah, some rebelled against the God ordained priestly order of Levitical priest. They wanted to change leadership. They were the first to try to change God's written laws. They wanted to rule the land their own way. God figured that since they wanted to rule Earth, He would just let them…so He opened up the ground and it swallowed them alive (Numbers 16:1-33). This, along with the golden calf incident, caused God to order the Israelites to move again. At Jericho, they lost faith in God who then ordered them to move around for forty years in the wilderness.

For forty days of rebellion God had sentenced the Israelites to forty years in the wilderness (Numbers 14:34). This in reality turned out to be a death sentence! A death sentence because all the adults except for Joshua and Caleb died during the forty-year circular march around the wilderness. The surviving children grew up in the wilderness and had children of their own, who also had children of their own. And there were a lot of them! These were the only Israelites ("Hebrews" by any other name) allowed to survive and enter the Promised Land (Joshua 5:6-7).

CROSSING THE JORDAN

When they had crossed the Jordan (on dry land) and conquered the Promised Land of Canaan, it was divided up among the twelve tribes of Israel. Each section was called by its Tribal name, i.e., Land of Gad, Land of Asher, Land of Dan, Ruben, Manasseh, and so on, but collectively it was all the "Country of Israel." For example, the Gadites were also Israelites. The Danites were also Israelites. And so on. Each group had their tribal and territorial title, but all were a part of the national identity of Israel as well.

Next, God (Yahweh) sent Judges to lead the nations (II Samuel 7:10). The nations were still under Levitical Law but from time to time needed further input. So God selected and sent Judges…a kind of mid-management concept. However, the people wanted to be more up-town, modern like all the other nations. "All the really cool nations had kings…so we want one too!" (I Samuel 8:5). They were not satisfied with the system God had set up for them. They wanted to change it. They desired a king so God sent them one. He sent them an emotional wreck named Saul.

DIVIDED KINGDOM

I'm not sure if God let them have a King out of anger---or as a joke---or as a lesson of some kind, but Kings they got. The first one was named King Saul. A King with some serious issues. So serious that a young shepherd boy named David had to come and play harp music to rid the King of evil spirits from God (see I Samuel 16:23). As it turned out, God had the Prophet Samuel anoint young David as the next King of Israel (I Samuel 16:12-13). Because of this, David spent a lot of time avoiding Saul.

Nevertheless after Saul's death David became King. David's first son died but his second one prospered under the LORD. This child was named Solomon. Solomon grew up to be King and under his rule, Israel prospered and remained, for the most, unified. However, after King Solomon's death the unified nation of Israel disagreed and split into two different nations: the Northern Kingdom held the name of "Israel" while the Southern Kingdom took the name of its majority tribe, "Judah."

Good enough? Nope! The Northern Kingdom just could not stand prosperity. They had to change worship. Their new King, an Ephraimite named Jeroboam, erected golden calves at the temples in Bethel and Dan for Israel's worship (I Kings 12:26-30). "Although not meant as idols but as pedestals for Yahweh, the calves became a syncrestic of Baal, which the bull is a symbol (Eerdman 568)."

To God, <u>idol worship is spiritual adultery</u>. Adultery, even spiritual adultery, is grounds for divorce and "divorce Israel" He did! "...when for all the causes whereby backsliding Israel committed adultery, I [God] had put her away, and given her a bill of divorce..."(Jeremiah 3:8). When God "puts away" a nation, they are gone...out of there.

He allowed her to be invaded, looted, people murdered and cities sacked and burned by Assyrian nations. The ten-tribes, which made up Israel (the Northern Kingdom), were no more! They were scattered throughout the world. Judah, the Southern Kingdom, was no angel either! Although God was offended by their behavior, He still spared them from vanishing. "The LORD was angry with Israel, and removed them out of his sight: there was none left but the tribe of Judah only...he had cast them out of his sight" (II Kings 17:18-20).

Judah was spared from extinction as a nation but still had to answer for their national sins. Later, God used the Babylonian empire to capture Judah's lands and burn the temple in their capital city of Jerusalem. A large portion of the Old Testament is devoted to this topic...especially the book of Daniel.

After about seventy years---the reign of four Kings---Judah was finally set free to return home and rebuild their capital city. (The book of Nehemiah tells of this rebuilding.) Although they were originally still <u>of</u> the Twelve Tribes of Israel, when Judah returned home they kept their national name of "Judah." Their Levitical based religion was still the religion of their ancestors, but because they were now the "nation of Judah," their religion was called "Judaism:" the religion of the "Jews." Now this brings us up to the time of Jesus.

<u>JESUS</u>

Born of Judah, a Jew and raised in Galilee, Jesus grew up on Judaism like those around him. When he started his pre-ordained ministry and taught his followers the new doctrine of Christianity (originally called "the Way") he altered the entire world. His followers wrote the 27 books of the *New Testament*, which is the dividing line between Judaism and Christianity.

> The living Messiah had come: "...the Lamb of God, which taketh away the sins of the world" (John 1:29) and He actually walked among men. The Apostle John tells us that it was actually God in the flesh, which walked among men:
>
> 1. "In the beginning was the Word, and the Word was with God, and the Word was God." 14. "And the Word was made flesh, and dwelt among us..." (John 1:1 & 14)

Many "came out" of Judaism and accepted this new thing called Christianity: this <u>denomination of the living Messiah</u>. They accepted that God had indeed put on flesh: been born of a virgin: preached the coming Kingdom: died on a cross at Calvary: on the third day rose from the grave: and eventually ascended into Heaven.

Jesus had taken <u>the religion of Adam</u> to a new level. He didn't change it---he enhanced it---made it clearer. He tried to "undo" all the damage four thousand years of man-made rules and tradition had done to God's Holy word. One might say that Jesus was the **first true Puritan**. He wanted to return to a <u>pure</u> worship of a pure God.

This purity is what the Sermon on the Mount is all about (see Matthew 5, 6, & 7). Jesus had been teaching the multitudes then withdrew to a mountain with <u>only</u> his disciples. "...he went up into the mountain, and when he was set, his disciples came to him"

(Matthew 5:1). There, uninterrupted, "He opened his mouth and began to teach them" (5:2). These twelve were to go out to the world, to a dying world, and spread the message of the Gospel. They were to clean up the mess that changes and false doctrine had made of God's Word.

In order to do this they first had to be "ordained." The Sermon on the Mount is their Ordination speech from Jesus.

> 13. "And he goeth up into a mountain, and called unto him whom he would, and they came unto him."
>
> 14. "And he ordained twelve that they should be with him, and that he might send them forth to preach." (Mark 3:13 & 14)

Later in John 20:22 Jesus gave them the Holy Ghost in order to empower them for this mission of the Gospel: "He breathed on them and gave them the Holy Ghost."

In the Sermon on the Mount, Jesus was instructing his disciples on what to expect. Of what to act like. Of what "to be." Today we call some of these instructions "the Beatitudes" (see Matthew 5:3-16). They are a lesson on what a Christian is "to be." Anything else is bogus and brings confusion.

The word of God had been so slanted by man that Jesus tried to explain it…explain how "it is about what is on the inside…not on the outside." How it is internal, not external. His statements such as "Ye have heard it was said by men of old…but I say to you…" are His bringing it back inside our hearts. He was NOT changing the law of God---just changing our focus point. He taught the twelve to get away from all the external distractions and desires and to turn inward. For example, he said to them:

> 27. "Ye have heard that it was said by them of old time, Thou shalt not commit adultery."

28. "But I say unto you, that whosoever looketh on a woman to lust after her hath committed adultery with her already in his heart." (Matthew 5:27-28)

All the man made changes deflected God's law from inside of us to the outside. From the heart to the outer world. To the things of the world instead of the things of the Spirit. He knew that God did not give a hoot about our looks, our wealth, our family or our church membership. God looks only at our hearts. At the essence of what we are!

7. "For the LORD seeth not as man seeth; for men looketh on the outward appearance, but the LORD looketh on the heart." (I Samuel 16:7)

Jesus taught, "Blessed are the pure in heart; for they shall see God" (Matthew 5:8). And the ancient commandment tells us to "... love the LORD thy God with all thine heart, and with all thy soul, and with all thy might" (Deuteronomy 6:5). "With all your heart" is the real message here! Paul even re-enforced this heart-thing when he wrote to the materialistic people of Rome:

9. "That if thou shalt confess with thy mouth the Lord Jesus, and hast believe in thine heart that God hath raised him from the dead, thou shalt be saved."

10. "For with the heart man beliveth unto righteousness: and with the mouth confession is made unto salvation." (Romans 10:9-10)

It's all about the heart! Every law of God is now written on our hearts (see I Peter 1:22), not in some Churches *Mission Statement* or *Charter of Beliefs*.

This "written on our hearts" is the Gospel in a nutshell! "...written not with ink, but with the Spirit of the living God, not in tables [tablets] of stone, but in fleshly tables of the heart" (II Corinthians 3:3). This is nothing really new to the worship of God. Even the Psalmist King David wrote of it in the *Old Testament*: "I delight to do thy will, O my God; Yea, thy law is written within my heart" (Psalm 40:8). And in 51:10 he sings, "Create in me a clean heart, O God; renew a right spirit within me."

This concept of "written on the heart," is the new covenant: God's law, His Word, written upon our hearts. It's internal---where it won't rust---where robbers can't steal it---and it won't be lost. That was Jesus' message to his Disciples! He didn't change anything other than what mankind had twisted around to fit himself. Jesus even became the Passover Lamb so that we might escape the sin-penalty of death. Even his death on the cross didn't change God's word: it fulfilled it and gave us a way out of this mess we made of things.

Christianity was built on the Word of God and fulfilled by Jesus. He is the cornerstone of our faith:

> 20. "And are built upon the foundation of the apostles and Prophets, Jesus himself being the chief cornerstone." (Ephesians 2:20)

This makes Christianity the "following of Jesus Christ and the belief that He is the Messiah...the living Savior." Of course, the Jews (those who practice Judaism) refused to accept Jesus, so they remained wrapped up in the practice of Judaism. Christianity had a long road ahead of it. It had the Jews on one side and the Roman Empire on the other. "Kill the children" had been Satan's cry from the early days of history and this new thing called "Christianity" was an infant.

With that in mind, for the next three-hundred years Christianity would be subject to all the growing pains and childhood illnesses of an infant. Out of this period, this time of newness, came the next major change: Constantine (288-337). Through this Emperor of Rome, our *Stew* was almost changed into something other than Christianity.

FORMATION OF THE ROMAN CATHOLIC CHURCH

A NOTE before continuing:

In Matthew 16:18 Jesus said to Peter (whose name means "Rock"): "...thou art Peter, and upon this rock I will build my church..." The Catholic Church claims to trace its roots all the way back to Peter. The Christian Church began in the New Testament days and was still there when Constantine organized the Roman faction and named it "Catholic." There is no historical record of the phrase "Catholic Church" before the fourth-century. So in this light, "yes," they can trace back to Peter and the Apostles...just like most other Christian Churches can. Constantine (as you will read in the following section) is the one who became a Christian and using his political influence Romanized it and presented it before the world. But this is not saying that the Catholic Church is the "only" church who can trace back to the apostles. All Christian Churches can.

Constantine became emperor of the greatest political and military force of the world: the "Roman Empire." He changed simple Christianity into something brand new. His creation of the Holy Roman Catholic Church (the R.C.C.) changed the flavor of the whole *Stew*. Its two main ingredients: "politics" backed by "military might," defined everything it did. (There are many good books on this topic, including E.G. White's *The Great Controversy*).

The Roman Empire was a true double-edged sword. It defended yet conquered. Created yet destroyed. Keeper of life, killer of the Saints. Holy yet Sinful. Both Christian and Pagan. We cannot forget that everything is a product of it is time and the Empire along with its offspring, the R.C.C., was no exception. It was the best and the worst of its time.

Time is the Great Tattletale. In its wake, many secrets are revealed. Biologist can look at the rings of a tree and discern with great accuracy years of drought and years of plenty. Geologist can look at strata (layers) of rock formations and pen point floods, fires, wildlife and even atmospheric pollutants of various times. Forensic Scientist gather bugs, a blade of grass, hair, dust and tissue samples and use them to reveal exact time of death and other investigative data. The same holds true for history: Christian history. We can look back at leaders, politics, conquest and even maps to determine with great accuracy the mode of the day. Was it a period of plenty? Of peace? Of war? Of conflict? A time of advancement or one of stagnation?

The stratum of American Christianity is thick and rich in history. It has four basic levels of deposits: 1) Adam to Jesus: 2) the Catholic Church: 3) American Colonialism: and 4) Modern Christianity. We have covered "Adam to the Cross," and now need to look at the mid-strata and determine how the formation of the Roman Catholic Church affected later deposits.

IV.

<u>FROM ROME TO PLYMOUTH ROCK</u>

In the fourth-century when Constantine created the Roman Catholic Church, mankind was in a "fallen condition." It was an age of War Lords, City States, changing creeds and violent Barbarism. Mother Rome, as it was called, had governed the western world but she was showing signs of decay. She was on her deathbed…she just had not lain down yet.

Her days of world power and glory were quickly fading. Vain

philosophies, political corruption, constant war, endless quest for riches, civil unrest and an un-yielding lust for power, all contributed to her fall. Since Rome was the "authority" of the day; the power that ruled mankind's daily life; the law that kept our violent barbarism in check and kept us from killing one another, she actually kept us alive. For this, we are grateful. She protected mankind from our own destructive nature. If Rome passed away so would civilization of the western world. Things were going to change and it would be a powerful change.

It started when the old emperor of Rome passed away, leaving no one to fill the empty throne. A battle began between a clever politician named Constantine and the General of the Roman army. Both wanted the empty throne! Constantine, being a shrewd politician, enlisted the help of the "common folk," while the General had only the army---which depended on the common folk for meals, horses, horse shoes, weapons, women and so on. Constantine promised the people freedom of religion if they'd help him win the throne. And help they did! They refused to serve the army. No food, lodging, weapons, women, and so on…all the things an army needed to function.

To top it off, in 312 AD, Constantine claimed to have seen a vision of a cross in the sky: "…in this sign we will conquer." Immediately, the cross was painted on his army's shield and banners. He won the battles and after claiming the throne issued his famous *Decree of Religious Tolerance*" (Rose 2). Rather than have an empire with dozens of opposing religions he combined them all into one neat and tolerant package. A "universal" religion for a universal empire. (The word "*Catholic*" means "universal" in Latin). This was the birth of the Roman Catholic Church: the *R.C.C.*

> "The movement [of Christianity] started the fourth century as a persecuted minority: it ended the century as the established religion of the empire. Thus, the Christian Church was joined to the power

of the State and assumed a moral responsibility for the whole society. To serve the State, it [Christianity] refined its doctrine… (Shelley 89)."

Now, according to the official teaching of the R.C.C. as defined in 1870 by the first Vatican Council, Jesus had established the papacy with the Apostle Peter. Eastern Orthodox Churches as well as all Protestant denominations deny these claims. For this reason, any study of the history of Christianity creates controversy, comparable to sticking our hand into a hornet's nest (Shelly 131).

Like it or not---accept it our not---the RCC, backed by Rome, took the reigns of fourth century Christian thought and shaped tradition for the next one-thousand years. Rather than a religion of blessings, it quickly became a political system of forced belief. One of conformity to the Church without exception! "By 380 [sometime between the Goth invasion of Rome and the Council of Constantinople] rewards for Christians had given way to penalties for non-Christians. In that year Theodosius made belief in Christianity an imperial command" (Shelly 96).

Like a raging grass fire, the R.C.C. blazed across Africa, Asia, and Europe. Wherever the Roman military went, it implanted its official religion. The Universal one. To defy the Holy Roman Church was to defy Rome itself! The growth of the Church was phenomenal! Shortly after its western spread and entrenchment in the world, the commanding empire of Rome folded and died. However, its Holy Roman offspring, the RCC, thrived to carry on the family name. It steadfastly became the sole representative of God on earth (Gallagher 6). From its conception, it carried the name of "Roman," and still carries it today.

Just as the ancient Israelites had the Mosaic Law and Levitical Priest to interpret God's rules of worship, the world had the Pope and his R.C.C. to do the job. Absolutely nothing happened unless the Church first approved it. No freethinking was allowed! To think outside the box---outside Papal dogma---was a heresy and punishable by death. The light of imagination was turned off. The Dark Ages had begun.

PAPAL AUTHORITY

During the thousand-year period between Constantine and 1350, the RCC metamorphosed into something else. It had taken itself a step further then just being the representative of God on earth. It had become a "god on earth." Follow its commands or die! It had succeeded in turning its <u>denomination</u> into a religion of its own. It became backed with the sword rather than by the *Bible*. The burning of Joan Arc in 1431 is a glowing example of this! Foxes *The Book of Martyrs* is filled with stories of this type of religious genocide. Remember, we are all a product of our time and the R.C.C. was no exception. However, time changes and with it so do men.

Two movements developed that freed man from the yoke of Catholicism: the Renaissance and the Protestant Reformation. Like brothers from the same parents, these two powerful movements are socially related yet unique and distinct individuals. Together they broke the hold the R.C.C. had on western civilization.

RENAISSANCE

Before the Renaissance, things had become violently oppressive. Science came to a crashing halt---even to hint that "the earth was not the center of the universe," was an act of heresy. Kings could not take the throne unless it was first approved by the Church. Because (it was decided that) all art belonged to its true creator (God), artists could not even sign their own work. Since the Church was decidedly God's representative on earth, if an artist did sign his own art he was blaspheming God by claiming the Churches property as his own. A rebellion evolved…starting with the artist and the free thinkers of the day.

This rebellion came to be known as the *Renaissance* (1400+). It, along with all its passion, came crashing through the darkness. People---creative people---wanted freedom of expression. This freedom, this drive to express ones creative self, lit up the Dark Ages like the noonday sun!

The word "*Renaissance*," means "rebirth." Western civilization had experienced a "new birth." A second chance to develop civilization without killing one another. The Church had carried humankind through barbarism and various other self-destructive life styles. Now it was time to loosen the reigns and see what man could do. Had he changed? Was this re-birth of the Renaissance a good thing? Had man changed for the better?

Man, during this transition period, had indeed changed. However, the Church had also changed…changed to a defensive posture. The idea of a loving God who extended mercy through His Son, Jesus, was put on hold while the Churches Inquisitional judges tried to put out the lights of the new freedom. Thousands died at the bloody hands of Inquisitional Judges for the crimes of Heresy, which was later declared "Witchcraft" (which allowed no defense at all).

Fortunately, the light of hope was still flickering in the smoke filled skies of the Dark Ages. "Let your light shine before men, that they may see your good works…" (Matthew 5:16). Like a searchlight ripping a hole through the night skies of Europe, Luther's "light could not be hidden." It was a signal light! It signaled in the next ingredient: "The Protestant Reformation." It would quickly change the flavor of the whole *Stew*.

REFORMATION

The year was 1517. The Renaissance had raised at least one generation of freethinking children. In response, the R.C.C. had already executed over three hundred thousand men, women and children for heresy or for the ridiculous crime of witchcraft.

(Robbens 4). This witch-burning period of Europe's history, from 1400 to 1712, is a testament to what can happen when man looks to a Church for direction rather than to God for direction. The R.C.C. had become as corrupt and oppressive as its deceased Mother Rome had before her demise.

One spring morning in 1515 a Catholic priest and teacher of German decent, named Martin Luther, had a soul transforming experience while reading the epistles of Paul. He had been taught, according to R.C.C. tradition, that Salvation was a mixture of faith in God---good works---obedience to the Church leaders---and the good works of one's local Church. He read Romans 1:17 (among others) "…and the just shall live by faith."

This revelation of "salvation by faith" and "not by works" jolted him to the core! It thrust him onto a path that would change the face of Christianity (Shelly 239). Luther saw it clearly: "If salvation comes through faith in Christ alone, the intercession of a priest is superfluous…the mediation of the Church of Rome crumbles into insignificance" (Shelly 240).

Two years later he completed his famous *"95 Theses."* It contained, in the final edit, 95 points showing where the R.C.C. was in scriptural error. He nailed it to the door of the Church in Wittenberg, effectively starting the "Protestant Reformation" (Shelley 240). His *Theses* called for an end to abuses such as priest selling indulgences and involvement in secular law (Rose 8).

His *Theses* was a type of Christ. It started a movement that would offer men the chance to be free from the bondage of man made wickedness. It was nailed to the Church just as effectively as Jesus was nailed to the Cross. The Church was no longer viewed as a protector of life but rather as executioner of the living. The Church (of this period) was a vivid example of "when good men make bad rules."

Pulled together under the Reformation movement, people

demanded change. They protested the administration of the Holy Office and of being forced, under threats of death, to worship the way the R.C.C. dictated. This earned them the title of *"Protesters,"* eventually termed simply "Protestants." Their movement was the Protestant Reformation and it is still moving today. It became the spicy, rich soup that flavored the other ingredients in our American *Stew* of Christianity.

PROTESTANISM

As with any revolt against authority, many "ideas" came to be voiced. Volumes upon volumes have been written about this period describing mountains of ideas and movements. Out of all this came three main Protestant camps:

1) the Reformist wanted to reform the Catholic Church:

2) the Puritans wanted to purify Christianity:

3) the Separatist wanted to separate totally from all established churches and start one's own.

All three were somewhat related, but still produced very different concepts of worship. All were Protestants, yet each held its own banner under which people could gather.

The R.C.C. was loosing its power too fast. But the big question was "could mankind pass the test?" Had he changed enough to govern himself without resorting to barbarism again? Could he keep his eyes on the Creator as he recreated himself without an army of Bishops, Cardinals, Popes and Canon Law to keep him in line? Many questions, but they were all growth questions.

It was like a child outgrowing his or her own clothes. Man had simply outgrown the R.C.C. He no longer needed his baby clothes. He no longer needed to be told every move to make or depend on others to tell him "how" to worship his God. He could handle it on his own now. He could pick out his own clothes: dress himself:

produce, achieve, survive his failures and strive for his success on his own. Most importantly though, man was mature enough now to decide his own goals and set his compass on his own. He would stumble and fall from time to time, but it was time to let go of the Mother's hand. (For more, see Luther in Index).

Of course, the R.C.C. felt threatened. They had already been executing people for hundreds of years for doing just what the Protestant Reformation was encouraging. Now it was time to accelerate the trials. Had to stop this Protestant thing! And the skies filled with smoke from the executional fires.

<u>BIBLE TRANSLATIONS (English)</u>

No amount of smoke could block the plan of God. He had a tremendous gift in store for the world. In the not-too-distant future, He would once again give His people (those of His Kingdom) an Ark. An Ark, which would hold His words---His laws---His expressed love for all mankind. This Ark would come in the form of the *King James Bible* (KJV). An English translation of God's Holy Word was the crowning product of the Protestant Reformation. It gave our *Stew* its robust flavor! No longer dependent on imports, England now had its own written Word of God.

Of course, the KJV wasn't the first or only English translation of the *Bible*. By 1381, John Wycliffe had already translated a good part of the *Latin Vulgate* into English. He was executed in 1384 but his suffering at the hands of the R.C.C. did not end at death's door. "In 1408 it became illegal to translate or to read the *Bible* in English without permission from a Bishop (Rose 8)." So in "1428 [40 years after Wycliffe's death] his body was exhumed and burned as a heretic" (Fox 68).

Without going into detail, the following is a list of some English translations before the 1611 production of the KJV:

1530 – *Tyndale Bible* –by William Tyndale.

1536 – *Coverdale Bible* – by Miles Coverdale.

1537 – *Matthew's Bible* – by John Rogers.

1539 – *Great Bible* – also by Miles Coverdale.

1564 – *Geneve Bible* – by Puritans in Geneva.

1568 – *Bishop's Bible* – by Matthew Parker.

1610 – *Rheims Bible* – by Gregory Martin.

All these were produced "after Martin Luther's 1517 *Theses*" (Walton 92).

These translations in English (not even counting the German, French, Spanish and other languages) show the great thirst for God's Word the Reformation exposed. "Blessed are they which do hunger and thirst after righteousness: for they shall be filled" (Matthew 5:6). History vividly shows that fear never successfully silences God's people. The Reformist, Separatists, and Puritans came forward in a seemingly endless supply of movements and ideas.

MARTYRS & MURDERS

These brave men and women, each an offspring of the union of the Renaissance and the Reformation, placed their freedom and faith in God's hands as they were martyred for their beliefs. Great men of faith such as:

William Tyndale arrested and burned at the stake in Brussels in 1536:

Hugh Latimer burned at the stake at Oxford in 1555:

John Hooper burned at the stake and dismembered in 1555:

Thomas Cranmer burned at the stake twice in 1556:

> Miles Coverdale, beaten to a cripple then exiled in1568:

In addition, many others gave their lives for the principles of worship according to the *Bible* rather than tradition (Walton 610). These deaths and all the other recipients of harsh treatment from the established Church witnessed first hand the effects of the churches "Counter Reformation."

Someone had to enforce the laws of the Church, and those that did were part of its Counter Reformation. This defensive tool of the R.C.C. had its own heroes of their faith as well:

> ---Reginald Pole put his life in jeopardy daily by dealing personally with Queen Mary Tudor of England (1500-1558):

> ---Robert Bellarmine opposed the teachings of Galileo and suffered beatings and mocking until his death (1542-1621;

> ---Peter Canisivs devoted his life to translating Catholic Catechisms into 12 languages and escaped death more than once (1521-1597):

And the many Kings, leaders and officials who willingly risk their lives and material goods to defend the honor of the RCC. All were devoted, through their faith in the Mother Church (Walton 68).

Remember, we are all a product of our time and place. They were too. However, with the martyring of countless Protestants and with the "free" circulation of the KJV, ultimately freedom won out. No man-made religion or political obstacles can stop people with a sincere desire to worship God. It didn't work for the Babylons against Daniel and his three friends. It didn't stop the Apostles of Jesus, and it didn't stop God's citizens in England either. Purity and

Truth led them out of oppression. "Thy word [Truth] is a lamp unto my feet and a light unto my path" (Psalm 119:105).

As stated earlier, Protestants came in three main categories: Reformist, Puritans and Separatist. Of course, history maintains dozens of other movements and camps of thought, but all came ultimately from one of these three Protestant groups.

<u>REFORMIST & ROYALTY</u>

First, let's look at the Reformist. They wanted to reform the Roman Catholic Church. It's rooted, ultimately, with King Henry VIII (1509-47) of England. He passionately desired the dark-eyed beauty, Ann Boleyn, a lady in waiting of the court. Problem was that the King was already married! Married to Catherine of Aragon---the daughter of Ferdinand and Isabella of Spain.

King Henry wanted a son and Catherine had only produced a daughter, Mary (later to become Bloody Mary when she takes over). Catherine had been the wife of Henry's deceased brother and in 1525 married King Henry. Since she had produced only a girl baby and the King wanted a son, Henry petitioned for divorce but the Church refused to give him one. Therefore, Henry used the *Bible*'s Leviticus 20:21 as grounds for divorce from Catherine. "And if a man take his brother's wife, it is an unclean thing…they shall be childless." Henry's position was that since Catherine had not given him a son, "they shall be childless" meant they "shall not produce a male child." In rebuttal, the RCC held its own saying "no." To them it meant "no children at all." But since they did have a child, Mary, it did not apply and no divorce would be granted. The Church of Rome refused to grant him a divorce.

In secret, Henry married Anne anyway. In May of 1533, he ordered an English secular court to declare his marriage to Catherine "null and void." He got his divorce! In September the new Queen Anne, gave birth to a baby girl they named Elizabeth. (Later they did have a son). Furious, the Pope moved to excommunicate the King. That's when King Henry had had enough! He realized that Papal authority in England had gone too far. It had to be overthrown.

He invoked a 14th century law, which prohibited dealings with "foreign powers," and the Vatican was, after all, a "foreign power." One year later, he confiscated all the Churches in England, stripping them of their coveted title of "Catholic," renaming them "The Church of England." He then declared himself "Defender of the Faith," and took over with the title of "Majesty of the Church." (Shelly 264)." He continued using most of the standard Catholic doctrine with the exception of "Papal authority." Authority, which now rested completely in the King's competent hands.

The King had a wandering eye and eventually divorced Ann and married a wealthy woman named Jane Seymour. Together they produced a son: Edward. After Henry's death in 1547 (thirty years after Martin Luther's *95 Theses* was nailed to the castle door in Wittenberg) his son took office. In 1553 young King Edward wrote an edit called "The 42 Articles of Faith" which defined the faith of the Church of England along Protestant lines (Shelly 269).

The same year that Edward died, his stepsister, Mary (Daughter of Henry and Catherine) took the throne and tried to dismantle Henry's Church of England along with Edward's Protestant ties to the Reformers. In four short years, she had over 300 Protestants burned at the stake, earning her the title of "Bloody Mary." Later, John Foxe collected reports on these deaths and included them in his famous book titled *"Foxes Book of Martyrs."*

In 1557, Bloody Mary, crippled and friendless, died a disappointed Queen. In steps the fiery headed Anne Boleyn's daughter, Elizabeth I (1538-1603). Elizabeth never liked the influence of Rome imposing itself on England so she worked hard to rebuild and strengthen the Church of England as a State controlled Church. She even changed her title from "Supreme Head" to "Supreme Governor." Elizabeth commissioned the *39 Articles of Faith* to be composed, which were essentially Protestant in ideology and tried to redefine a State Church people would honor. Her *"Via Media,"* or "Middle Way," was a blend of State law and God's law. Out of this the Church of England grew strong and independent of Roman influences (Shelly 370).

This is exactly what the Reformers wanted. A reformed Church in which to worship. The idea, or concept, of a reformed Church went out through all of Europe. It, along with Luther's book, *"The Babylonian Captivity of the Church,"* spread like wild fire and showed that the bondage of oppression not only "should be broken," but that it "could be broken." As influential as it was, there remained many who still felt that the Church was beyond reform---beyond repair. They wanted a pure religion---for a pure God.

PURITANS

These Puritans became a force in world history themselves. Although the title "Puritan," wasn't official until 1566 (World Book Vol. 15, p 803) it was a common belief reaching back before Luther. The force they rallied around came in the form of a Frenchman. A Frenchman named John Calvin (1509-1564).

Calvin was a man of his day. As Luther's doctrine was "justification by faith alone," Calvin's was "the Sovereignty of God alone" (Shelly 257). John Calvin asserted that all Church organization and government should come from the *Bible* itself and each congregation should be independent and free to choose its own Pastor (World Book Vol. 15, p 803). Calvin was forced to flee Paris into Geneva where he led the Swedish Reformation in 1541. Protestant refugees from all over Europe came to Geneva under the banner of Puritan Calvinism (Walton 55). This title would carry on for years to come, even until today. (For more see, Mayflower in INDEX).

NOTE: not all Puritans were Calvinist but all Calvinist were Puritans. Some of the non-Calvinist drifted toward the Separatist movement.

SEPARATIST

Out of the kingships of Henry VIII, all the way to James I (formerly James VI of Scotland) a group of unsatisfied believers voiced their unrest with the Church of England. They felt---for assorted reasons---that the Church still had too much Catholic dogma in it, making it too far gone to be salvaged. They separated themselves from all established Churches and formed small "cell" groups known as "Separatist groups" (Shelly 293-295).

By 1611 James I, the son of Mary, Queen of Scotts, finally ordered a new translation of the *Bible*. This was a Separatist dream! No more half translations. No longer dependant on the Catholic's *Latin Vulgate*. Now, at last, England had a full English translation "authorized" and financed by the King himself. It was reliable, accurate, used the worlds of the day, and best of all: it was affordable. Even the poor could own a copy of God's written *Word*.

King James---remember, his mother was Mary of Scotts (Bloody Mary) ---was not as zealous about the Reformation and Counter Reformation as his mother had been. He was more concerned with politics, drinking, and civil law, so his next act was to dissolve Parliament. For the next ten-years, he ruled England without a Parliament. This single act opened the doors of the established Church of England, and allowed Separatist, all those who wanted to separate from the Church, to flee in huge numbers (Shelly 295).

Many, now without Parliamentary rule to hinder them, were free to band together and leave England altogether. They fled to Holland, Germany, and even to Austria to organize "homes of worship" patterned after their own beliefs. One such man was John Smyth.

His main platform, taken from the New Testament, was the argument concerning infant baptism verses Immersion. He preached that infant baptism was not an act of faith; therefore, it was not scriptural (Shelly 296). In 1609, in Amsterdam, Smyth along with forty congregation members professed their faith in Jesus Christ and were baptized. This was, for the record, the first English speaking Baptism by immersion.

In the meantime, Dutch, Spanish, French, Portuguese and English explorers had mapped and claimed parts of the New World: America. This had to have been God's timing. It was just too perfect! Too right on time! His people needed somewhere to go…and He was providing it.

THE MAYFLOWER

Thousands of Protestants from all ideologies dreamed of a land---a free land---where they could worship and love the LORD in the way His Spirit directed them. A land free from death at the hands of Inquisitional trials. A land free from egotistical Kings and bloody Queens. A land free from unstable Secular Laws that changed with the political winds…here today, gone tomorrow. As providence would have it, they saw just such a land in America.

Remember, King HenryVIII had outlawed Catholicism in England, so England was about the only European country any Protestants (especially Separatist) could live in free from any Catholic Inquisitional trials. England, jolly old England, needed people to settle the New World and found them in the Protestants. They were packed and ready to go!

Armed with their *King James Bibles* (Shelly 294), suited up in the full armor of God (Ephesians 6:11-17), filled with the courage to tame a new land, and with hearts bursting with hope and guided by the Holy Spirit of God, the Protestant settlers boarded ships and set sail for the New World.

Puritans, Separatist, Reformers, Anabaptist and Rebaptizers, all were proud to claim the task of reinstating purity to Christian worship. For this reason most historians called them all Puritans, and because of their pilgrimage from Europe to America they earned the secular title of "Pilgrims." One such group of these Pilgrims, celebrated as the first to set sail for America to settle, was aboard a ship named the "Mayflower." (World Book Vol. 15, p 419). Due to harsh wind and new seas, the Mayflower drifted off course and landed along the desolate coast of Cape Cod, Massachusetts.

On December 21, 1620, the Pilgrims stepped on shore. They realized they had to face harsh times but still they stayed. On Sunday, January 21, 1621, led by William Brewster, they conducted the first Protestant service in the New World (Murrell 135). What an honor Pastor Brewster held. Leading this very first service on American soil!

When the Mayflower had first dropped anchor in the choppy waters of the Bay, the anchor had not gone down alone. With it had dropped the heavy yoke of Inquisitional Catholicism and oppression from selfish royalty. The Plymouth Bay had served as a symbolic Baptizing: it cleansed away the dogma and harsh Canon Law from the lives of the settlers. The name "Pilgrim" became synonymous with "Puritan," symbolizing the journey of those souls driven by a desire for Pure Christianity. That day their denomination became "Pilgrim."

By 1640, almost 21,000 colonists were living in the vicinity. A congregational form of government was adopted. Within ten years, 33 assemblies existed in Massachusetts alone. Denominations thrived under this form of government, leading to various forms of ecclesiastical government systems thrown into the Great *Stew* being assembled. For example:

EPISCOPAL	Jamestown, VA, Salem and Boston, MA, Charleston, SC
CONGREGATIONAL	Plymouth, MA

DUTCH REFORMED NY, Camden, NJ	Albany & New Amsterdam,
BAPTIST	Providence, RI
QUAKERS	Philadelphia, PA
MORAVIANS	Bethlehem, PA
MENNONITE	Lancaster & Germantown, PA

(Murrell 135)

It had been quite a journey for Christianity. It had been formed in Judea by Jesus---spread by the Apostles---taken over by Rome---twisted by politics---energized by the Renaissance---freed by the Reformation---and delivered to American shores on the Mayflower. The Great *Denominational Stew* was boiling. Was it time to add more ingredients? Time to Americanize it!

Add generous amounts of freedom; strong willed people; love for God; and an extreme caution of any organized religion that tries to impose its rules on God's children. Would America be the birthplace of their dream of pure worship? All the ingredients were there...waiting to be put into the pot.

A NOTE ON THE REFORMATION

This is not at all implying that Luther's *Thesis* nailed to the door of Wittenberg Castle (1517) was the sole cause of the Reformation. It had only been the blasting cap, which ignited the movement. A movement, which had been evolving into a powder keg for several hundred years. Of course, I cannot include all the people and events, which contributed here, it would take a thousand pages to detail all the contributions made. Below is just a sampling of some of them:

The Paulicians focused on the epistles of Paul and have been around since the 7th century.

The <u>Bogomils</u> were an outgrowth of the <u>Excites</u> and rejected all sacraments.

> A small group called <u>Catherine</u> rejected sacraments but also opposed marriage, purgatory, and swearing vows. Many more were burned at the stake for refusing to accept the Inquisitional Court's authority.

> The <u>Waldensians</u> encouraged lay preachers and even permitted women preachers. Founded in 1215 by Peter Waldo of France, they were persecuted and executed but several survived until 1512 when they joined the Puritans during the Reformation.

The <u>Lollards</u> also encouraged lay-preachers, denied transubstantiation, purgatory and priestly celibacy, gained early Pre-Reformation fame when they adopted Wycliffe's teachings. They were almost exterminated as martyrs! Their leader, Sir John Oldcastle, was said to have been Shakespeare's model for the character of Flagstaff.

The <u>Hussites</u> also denied transubstantiation and veneration of the saints. Followers of John Huss, they split many times under many names: <u>Taberrtes</u>, <u>Utraquist</u>, <u>Unitas</u> and the <u>Bohemian Brethren</u>.

> Influenced by the <u>Waldensians</u>, many of these united and formed the <u>Moravian</u> Church, which was a pillar of Reformation theology and the global missionary field.

Like a long buried treasure, the chest had to be ripped open with force and each precious piece cleaned and presented before the people…the rightful owners of the treasure.

Issues such as original sin, free will, predestination, atonement, grace, works verses faith, regeneration, justification, sacraments, Hell and Heaven, had to be re-examined and compared to scripture. Other more "legal" matters arose and had to be rehashed and presented to the public as well: repentance, baptism, the Lord's Supper, Church and State relations, priestly orders verses elected preachers, and even sin and Godly behavior had to be cleaned up. Quite a job! And it's still going on today.

Ever since the RCC imposed itself on Christianity there has been unrest among the ranks of the Saved. But every movement has its Hero and history has declared, hands down, Martin Luther as that hero and champion of the faith. None of the great Confessions: the *Schleitheim Confession* (Swill Anabaptist 1527): the *Augburg Confession* (German Luthern in 1530): the *Terrapolitan Confession* (German Reformed in 1531): the *Helvetic Confession* (Swiss Reformed in 1536): the Galliacan, Scors, Belgie, and even the *Huguenots Confession*, would have been likely without Luther's bold leadership. "Creeds and Confessions" quickly became the dominate thought of Christian life during the Reformation.

Though the Catholic against Protestants: the Reformist verses Counter-reformation: and the Lutherans competing against Reformed; the Word of God has survived and guided people as a testament of His Will. It has overcome greed, corruption, and the bloody hand of Inquisitional Courts. It has survived to be OUR beacon in an otherwise darkened sea. And we are humbled under the mighty hand of God, that "He may exalt you in due time" (I Peter 5:6). And exalt us He did! America, with Christianity as its backbone, feeds the world, and through Christian Missionaries we bring the Gospel of Jesus Christ to "all nations" (see Matthew 28:19).

Yes, God Has exalted this land as a Great Nation. He planned for us, perpetuated our growth, propelled us to industrial expertise, powered us as the academic Capital of the world, and instilled in our hearts the noble position as that "City on the Hill," all for the glory of our LORD and Father.

The Reformation was His idea. Not ours! Nevertheless, it now rest in our hands to protect and to nurture the way the Creator guides us. When the Pilgrims reached the New Land, I'm sure that they, just like Moses did, took their shoes off. The following poem by Elizabeth B. Browning hangs in my office as a reminder of God's glory around us:

Earth is crammed with Heaven,

Every flower is ablaze with the fire of God.

Those who see, take their shoes off...

The Rest just pick flowers.

The early settlers---the seed planters of today's denominations---were NOT just picking flowers. They were on their knees thanking God for their sight! They could see God at work in their lives. They knew that the future of Christianity was in their hands and in their decisions about the future of worship. Their purity is the character of our *Stew*. Nevertheless, somewhere along the way it got over-seasoned. This next section will show how it came about.

PART TWO
Developing an American Christianity

V.

THE STRUGGLE FOR IDENTITY

The word is "Ecumenical." It means "worldwide" or "all included." When applied to Christianity it implies a oneness in faith. "One Lord, one faith, one baptism" (Ephesians 4:5). This has been called "the spirit of unity" and taught throughout God's Word. Is this unity---this ecumenical condition---a way of life, or only the goal of one's Christian practice? Are all alike or can we be different, yet still ecumenical?

On very few subjects do all men think alike? Certainly, Christians do not all think the same way about their faith. They have differences about doctrines, mortality, baptism, worship, and church organization. Their views are not mere opinions but a religious conviction based on an interpretation of scripture. As a result, Christians disagree over a good number of areas about "what Christianity is." Some defend their denominational distinctions. Others call them a sin and a scandal. In either case, ecumenicity is one of the hallmarks of 20th century Christianity (Shelly 442).

This ecumenicity, this unity in practice, was paramount in the minds of the early settlers to America. They had come looking to build a utopia "under God," but instead were often met with hardships, famine, death, hostile attacks and divided interpretations of scripture among different groups.

Utopian ideas were nothing new. Virgin land and Freedom of Religion seemed to nurture that dream despite the hardships. America had its share of failed utopian communities over the years:

> The "Order of the Solitary" in Ephrate, PA (1698-1750):
>
> The "United Society of Believers in Christ Second Appearing" in Lebanon, NY and Union Village, OH (1780-1796):
>
> The "Society of the Public Universal Friends" in Lake Seneca, NY (1780-1819):
>
> The "Harmony Society" in Harmony, IN and in Economy, OH (1780-1847):
>
> and many others (Walton 97). All failed experiments in their times.

Experiment or not, what really defined American Christianity was its odd mix of variety based on unity. Ecumenicalism through diversity! Is this an oxymoron? Nope. The early Americans were only sixteen-hundred years out of step with the Church, which Jesus founded in the first Century. They could either walk backwards in time to unravel the doctrines of men and those of God as the Reformist had tried to do, or start over anew as the Separatist had. Both in unity with their search for purity in worship, yet different in their methods to reach that purity. It was variety based on unity. Out of this came the unique phenomenon of American Denominations.

This movement was radically new to the world. Imagine a country where it was actually "ok" to question Church doctrine and tradition! Edward C. Wharton, author of the text *The Church of Christ,*

The Nature of The New Testament Church, defines denominations as, "A doctrinally distinct body of professed Christians who have denominated themselves with a distinctive name by which they distinguish their characteristic doctrine" (Wharton 53). In this sense, scriptural interpretation, sound or not, essentially defines the denomination. Reasoning based on specific interpretations produces the meat for our *Denominational Stew*.

This brings us to the next phase of developments: "The Age of Reason." Up until this point Church selection had been an escape from forced worship but now, once settled in the New World, folk could take time to contemplate nature, science, and the mysteries of God. "Come, let us reason together," was the cry of the day. No longer would it be a choice based on emotion or fanaticism, but one based on reason and logic. A New Christianity---a thinking man's religion---planned and proper!

This gave stability to our *Stew*. Like when cooking spaghetti and the boiling water starts to spill over the lip of the pot…just pour some vegetable oil on the rolling water and it will hold it down a bit. It will stop water from boiling over the edge! "Reason" worked much the same way to the freed believers. It did not lower their flame of zeal, but only held it down to a controlled boil… wouldn't let it spill over. It kept unity prevalent among believers, yet encouraged the freedom to question. This "reason," this logical approach to Christianity, is the key ingredient to the next phase: the "Age of Reason."

VI.

THE AGE OF REASON

Colonial America came into its first real "change in thinking" around the turn of the 17ᵗʰ Century. Historians bracket the period 1648 to 1789 as the Age of Reason in America. And reason they did! With no earthly authority to tell them what to think, they were in the cherished position of being able to do their own thinking. To reason things out for themselves.

Of course, reasoning wasn't new. It's the natural evolution to the next step after settling down somewhere. Its like after moving into a new house it takes some time to get settled in. Then comes "the change." Buy new furniture: do some painting: plant new grass: change it up a little…anything…just change things around. That's what we humans do. We add to or change things. To the Colonial Settlers the "big change" came in a European package called "The Age of Reason." It changed American Christian thought drastically! This new period was a true double-edged knife. Reason could create or destroy. It taught reason over superstition, thus bringing enlightenment while destroying comfort. It welcomed dialectic debate over previously taboo subjects. It encouraged respect for science over myth and custom. "Human reason all but replaced the Christian faith as the cornerstone of Western culture." (Shelly 309). Freedom and Reason: the freedom to think and to voice your conclusions, gave license to "look into" and to "inspect" the logic of it as well. God had already cautioned man about mind reading the Creator:

> "For my thoughts are not your thoughts, neither are your ways my ways, saith the LORD. For as the

heavens are higher than the earth, so are my ways higher than your ways, and my thoughts than your thoughts." (Isaiah 55:8-9).

It became fashionable to reason-out one's religious opinions and even to devise one's own new ideas about creation, heaven, salvation, morality, and so on. Newness through reason became the rage of the day. Bruce Shelley, the author of, *Church History In Plain Language,* writes, "The age of reason was nothing less than an intellectual revolution, a whole new way of looking at God, the world, and one's self. It was the **birth of secularism**" (Shelley 312). Although rooted in Europe's Age of Reason, the American version was steeped in Christianity: the reason of faith, of the church, of government, marriage, and so on down the list.

Yes, it drew focus on science and logic over traditional beliefs, but the new Americans wanted to separate from tradition anyway. So it fit right in! It gave them a head start while the flurry of a new government was being constructed. Rather than building a nation of scientific atheist, it actually grounded them firmly in great *Bible* Truths. God's Word cannot be reasoned away so easily. Its power and Truth have stood the test of time.

To demonstrate the enormous power of Reason (which the Creator instilled in humans) Frank S. Mead, co-author of *The Handbook of Denominations*…writes: "A disproportionate number of Nobel Peace Prize winners have been people whose religious convictions led them to confront injustice and seek to reconcile warring enemies" (Mead 15).

True science seeks only to understand the physical laws that God created and how to use them. There are as many false scientists out there as there are false preachers. False in the sense that they slant data (or twist scripture) for their own personal gain…to say, "See what I have discovered!" Whereas, truth-seeking Christian and truth-seeking Scientist seek truth for truth's sake alone. Pure truth is its own reward. A true man of God and a true Scientist have more in common than most realize.

For this cause, through logic and new scientific thinking, the face of a growing America was changed. Change was seen in its colleges and universities: in its new government after the war with Britain: and in the sermons delivered from denominational pulpits. Like a vaccination against some growth-stunting disease, reason, logic and freedom of religious expression surged through America's veins and destined her to grow into a world super power. Growth itself became the next ingredient in our Great *Stew of Denominationalism*.

"Anyone who could gather followers could be the founder of a new denomination" (Mead 17), and contribute to America as a reasoning, Christian super power. So create denominations they did! The "trick," if that's the right word, to forming a new denomination in early America was to present one's message in a logical manner that appealed to current issues and to potential members. No longer were people forced under threats of death to follow established doctrine and rules of worship. Nevertheless, under the protection of "reason" they could choose which service to attend. Logic was the new King.

Prove your case through logic and reason and no one would dare to stop you. If a new group worshipped in the manner that you reasoned was correct, join them and accept their name---their denominational name---the name they group under. This process is still with us today. Church hopping is as American as apple pie. Recruitment and competition took off like a rocket!

Free competition made American Christianity unusually responsive to changes in society as denominations adopted popular culture, especially music, for attracting members. Each generation has seen the creation of new religious bodies and the transformation of older bodies just to "sell" members and potential members on their "new way." Interesting that Jesus called himself "the Way…" (John 14:6).

Along with freedom of religious expression came another benefit of colonizing a new land: "free enterprise." Once economic bonds were broken with England the potential for wealth in America was reasoned by many as a sign that God was showing them favor. This "favor" in wealth was called Divine Providence and was seen as uncontestable proof that God was with them. Divine Providence became the outward proof of God working inside of a particular person, family, community or church. This "pocketbook expression" of an inward experience attracted many seekers to America's shores and, like it or not, it is still with us today in the Word Faith Movement (also called "The Emerging Church").

This "wealth-is-the-proof" concept is the platform of many televangelist and prosperity preachers today. They teach the "name it and claim it" message which is in reality sorcery masquerading as Christianity. It teaches that all believers are little gods who can speak things into existence. This type of teaching is dangerous because it moves worship away from God and focuses it on man (self). To demonstrate this "we are gods" message the following is a segment of a conversation between Paul & Jan Crouch and Kenneth Copeland (three of the biggest names in the "name it and claim it" arena). It was taken from a broadcast of the Trinity Broadcast Network's program "Praise The Lord."

> PAUL: God doesn't even draw a distinction between Himself and us.

> KENNETH: Never! You never can do that in a covenant relationship.

> PAUL: Do you know what else that has settled tonight? …the controversy that has been spawned by the devil to try and bring dissension within the body of Christ that we are gods. I am a little god.

43

KENNETH: Yes! Yes!

JAN: Absolutely. He gave us His name.

PAUL: I have His name. I'm one with Him. I'm in a covenant relationship---I am a little god!

KENNETH: You are anything that He is.

PAUL: Yes. That's it exactly.

This Word Faith teaching is powerful and puts men equal with God. Is it illogical? Unreasonable? It in itself is proof that men's logic can be flawed and how easily our personal desires (lust of the eyes, lust of the flesh, and pride of life...1 John 2:16) can pervert our power of reason. Look at what happened to Eve when she desired to be like God (Genesis 3:6 & 16).

Isn't it odd that something as unreasonable as this took place way back in America's Age of Reason? It was during this period of wealth---of Divine Providence---of wide-open spaces and wide-open dreams---that men's minds were freed to reach out. This brought an explosion of ideas and theologies.

This period of governmental questions and religious drive pulled people together into what was effectively the beginning of many movements that still exist today in America. Theology was the next frontier to explore! While all this new thinking and new marketing was forming as the country spread to the west, the concept of American Christianity itself became distinct and emerged in three distinct stages: 1) the First Great Awakening; 2) the Second Great Awakening: and 3) the Age of Media Christianity. But first, we need to look at the ways men viewed the Sovereignty of God. After all, isn't God the one in charge of His religion? Is His will strong enough to keep man from altering what He established?

VII.

THE SOVERIGNTY OF GOD

The word "sovereignty," in a secular sense, according to *Webster's Dictionary*, means "a supreme ruler or monarch: supreme in rank, power, or authority: having independence" (p 687). When used in a theological sense, according to *Nelson's Bible Dictionary*, it "refers to the unlimited power of God who has sovereign control over the affairs of nature and history" (1196). He suggests reading Isaiah 45:9-19 and Romans 8:18-39.

There is only one sovereign God: Yahweh, the God of Israel, the Creator, or "the Father" as Jesus liked to refer to Him. He has tried to bring this message to mankind from the beginning. He created us (Genesis 1:27): He gave us life (Genesis 2:7): sent His own Son to redeem us from our sins (Titus 2:14): and sent His very own spirit, the Holy Ghost to teach us (Luke 12:12): and to empower us (Acts 1:8): all because God loves us (see John 3:16). All this is possible because He is the Sovereign God over all creation: over both seen and unseen creation. "His will be done," is the creed of His *Bible*. His will cannot help but to become reality. It will happen!

But what about man's will? What about that part we call "freewill?" Can what we choose, by exercising our power of free will, to over-ride God's will? This is a serious question. If God's will is for all to be saved, "…not willing that any should perish, but that all should come to repentance" (II Peter 3:9), then the sacrifice of Jesus is not needed because no one can be lost. God "willed" everyone to be saved so we will be. This can't be! We don't have the freewill to choose or to refuse God's will do we? With every choice there are consequences!

The other side is that God offers salvation to all who willingly believe and accept it (John 11:26, Romans 10:9, and others). Only the ones who willingly accept His terms will be saved. So what about those called the "elect?" (See Matthew 24:22, Mark 13:27, and others). Those He "predestinated" to be saved (see Romans 8:29, Ephesians 1:11, John 15:16 and others). He chooses some, the "elect," to be saved, but what about the rest of mankind? See the problem here? This raises all kinds of questions!

Out of this came two great camps of theological debate: "Calvinism" and its near opposite, "Arminianism." The main concern of each is not so much the issue of baptism, *Bible* translations, covenant laws and such, but are totally absorbed with the paradigms of God's Sovereignty and man's freewill. How much---what are the limits---and by which are we saved?

So before continuing on our journey of American *Denominational* Stew, we pause for a moment and inspect these two main ingredients: Calvinism and Arminianism. They are the two biggest players in the game now.

CALVINISM

Perhaps no other reformer did so much to force people to think about Christian ethics as did John Calvin (1509-1564). The son of a lawyer for the Catholic Church in Neyan, France, John studied Greek and Latin at the University of Paris. It was there, in Paris in 1533, that he joined the ranks of the Protestants and moved to Geneva.

Deeply influenced by German leaders, especially those from Strasbourg, John devoted his life to Christian thought and social reform. His influence grew almost overnight to engulf the whole of Europe. Those who followed him were called "Calvinist" and the teaching was "Calvinism."

Calvinism agrees with most other Reformation leaders on such basics as the superiority of faith over works: the *Bible* as God's inspired writings: the priesthood of believers: and Jesus is the way to salvation. Where his Calvinism makes its stand is in the proposition that men are "saved" <u>solely</u> by the "election" of God. That it is God's sovereign will and there is nothing man can do to over-ride it! We cannot "choose" salvation---it's already reserved for His elect...only His elect. We cannot exercise our "will" over what God has already chosen. Calvinism follows a simple five-point system known by the acronym T.U.L.I.P.

T = men are totally depraved…

U = God's elect have unmerited/undeserved favor…

L = Grace is limited to only His elect…

I = grace is irresistible…they will be saved…

P = Perseverance of the Saints…

Out of Calvin's ideas on politics and social reform, he developed the system of church government that today is called "Presbyterian" (World Book vol 3, p 58-59). Based on Calvin's teachings that "the elect were chosen before the foundation of the world," (taken from Ephesians 1:11), people "reasoned" that the doctrine of Divine Providence (meaning that surely God would also provide for and protect His elect) is evidence in itself exactly "who are His chosen ones." It must be those who prosper!

In application, having a safe journey to America and prospering in an untamed land was proof positive through Divine Providence that one was an elect. Naturally, this caught on like wildfire in America. Prosperity and health was proof of God's election---while poverty and illness was proof that one was "not" one of God's elect. (We still see this type of thinking in many Christians today).

This side of Calvinistic Providence was imported to America by the Puritans and salted our Stew with hope and with confidence in God's grace. God had indeed "shed His Grace on Thee…" The following old Hymn by Peter Eldersveld, expresses the Calvinistic view of election:

> *T'is not that I did chose Thee,*
> *For, LORD, that could not be.*
> *This heart would still refuse Thee,*
> *Hadst Thou not chosen me?*
> *Thou from the sin that stained me,*
> *Hast cleansed and set me free:*
> *Of old, thou hast ordained me,*
> *That I should live to Thee.*

(Chapel Library 8)

The whole of Calvinist philosophy was that God is in charge---He made all the rules---He and He alone selected the Saints---and He prospered them so others would know that these were His children. God was 100% sovereign. His will was supreme! *"Tis not that I did chose Thee---For LORD, that could not be."* But what about those NOT chosen by God? Were they born to go to Hell's fire? Were they doomed without hope of salvation? See the problem for a budding nation where "all men are created equal?"

True to the concept of predestination, this question was addressed even before it was ask. It had been addressed by a man named Jacobus Arminius.

ARMINIANISM

Named for the Dutch Calvinist, Jacobus Arminius (1560-1609), the doctrine generally became a liberal alternative to the rigid belief of High (or hyper) Calvinism in predestination. Arminius, who studied in Geneva at the University of Leiden believed that, like Calvin had, God had pre-selected some persons for heaven and others for Hell as indicated by Jesus' reference to "sheep and goats" (Matthew 25:32). But he focused almost entirely on the Love of God rather than on predestination of the elect.

One year after his death a group of ministers who sympathized with his views developed a systematic theology based on his teachings of God's love and mercy for all men. They argued that Grace could be rejected; that Christ intended that it was possible for all persons to be saved; and it was possible to be saved and then fall away from God's Grace and Salvation. Man's choice to choose by exercising his "freewill" was entirely in the hands of the individual himself. He could choose to accept or to reject God. Man's gift of freewill was what was "made in the image of God" in Genesis 1:27.

This movement had its ups and downs and wasn't fully accepted until the British Theologian, John Wesley (1703-91), affirmed the work of Arminius in his Methodist movement during the 18th century in England. What he went by was a document named "*The Remonstrance*," which was signed by 45 ministers who had been trained earlier by Arminius himself. The document (and copies of it) was later exported to America as the theology of the "Remonstrates," which is just another name for Arminianism (Murrell 105).

The document became the written bases for Arminianism in America. It promoted belief that no predestination exist and people, all people, are free to accept or to reject the Gospel and salvation (Funk & Wagnell vol 2, p 368). The Arminianistic theology can be explained in five steps:

1) That Christ loves every individual and desires that all be saved.

2) Jesus offers salvation to all but many refuse to come to it.

3) Jesus cannot regenerate a sinner who does not of his own free will choose to be saved.

4) The death of the Savior was in vain unless you accept it for yourself. By non-acceptance, you are lost. It's your choice.

5) Once you accept Jesus and His sacrifice for your sins, you can later fall away from the faith.

Salvation is not based on God's will or on your works, but is based on your free choice and through a variety of reasons you can change your mind at a later date and return to being un-saved if you so choose.

As one can see, Arminianism is a far cry from the message of Calvinism. It's pleasing to hear and was a handy alternative to it. A bright side was that the Arminianian position seemed perfect for the improvised and sick settlers for whom Calvinism's brand of Divine Providence deemed un-savable. Arminianism was exactly what was ordered for the ill and those deemed "savages." It accepted all, regardless of health, wealth, race, creed or color. Naturally, this was popular teaching in the land of the free. Its heart is reflected in Emma Lazarus poem, "The New Colossus," which hangs near the Statue of Liberty at the gateway to our Land of the Free:

"Give Me Your Tired, You're Poor,

You're Huddled Masses, Yearning to be Free.

The Wretched Refuse

of Your Teeming Shores."

This sounds like something Jesus would say. "Send me those who need me!"

Arminianism is the Sweetener in our Stew. It adds a touch of sweetness, whether it is artificial sweetener or real sugar, the effect is the same. The debate is still raging on over which is scripturally correct. We will cover this more in detail in a later section. Like the comedian, Jackie Gleason used to say, "How sweet it is!"

VIII.

THE FIRST GREAT AWAKENING

"The greatest manifestations of Divine Grace in the history of the Church are those times when the LORD visits His people in a mighty way" (Murrell 142). During the short period known as the First Great Awakening, "God used the power of His own Word [through traveling Evangelist] to frustrate the works of the Devil…Souls were snatched from the jaws of destruction by those powerful preachers of righteousness" (Murrell 142, 143). This was the wake-up call for the American settlers! Once they were settled in and comfortable, God's alarm clock went off. The First Great Awakening stirred men's souls and jolted them awake.

It's difficult to narrow an "idea" down to a specific date, but most agree that this "First Great Awakening" in America was from 1730 to 1744. It was the beginning of a love affair Americans will develop with revival. It was filled with legendary men of God such as, William Tennent, Jonathan Edwards, and Theodore Frelinghysen whom George Whitfield called "the beginner of the great work" (Shelley 745). These powerful preachers criss-crossing the land with impassioned appeals for repentance became prime factors in developing the character of our Great *Stew*.

Under their voice, Americans came to know both the frown and the smile of God. "It [the Awakening] restored both the tears of repentance to colonial Christianity and the joy of salvation" (Shelley 745). They believed, through the designs of Divine Providence that God had smiled upon their quest for liberty. The First Great Awakening was God revealing His approval upon men.

One such man whose light held legendary brightness throughout the Connecticut River Valley of those early 1700's was the Hellfire and Brimstone preacher named Jonathan Edwards. His powerful voice and fiery style of persuasion woke people from their sleep. He had been described as "merciless" in his preaching style. When he preached about *"Sinners in the Hands of an Angry God,"* he would describe God firmly holding men over the flames of Hell in a way one held a loathsome spider over a candle. He would vocalize how it would feel to have the searing agony of a burn drawn out through eternity! He told listeners how the ground under their feet was rotten flooring over a blazing pit, ready to give way any second. Sobs and gasps rose from the crowds to such levels he had to pause at times...his voice being drowned out by theirs (Shelley 364).

Another voice, one that couldn't be drowned out swept over Georgia, Virginia, Maryland, Pennsylvania and the Carolinas like a spiritual hurricane. It was the booming voice of the Great Revivalist, George Whitefield. His impassioned lectures are still studied in seminaries today. He eventually drifted northward winning the admiration of politicians and common people alike.

In Philadelphia, he even captured the respect of the worldly-wise Benjamin Franklin with his *"Men are Assuredly Half Beast and Half Devil"* sermon. It explained to the deistic Franklin God's purpose for men in this land of Providence. Out of this developed the position that a nation could indeed be devotes of one God but not under the authority of one State Church. "The fundamental belief that God has appointed two different kinds of government [civil and ecclesiastical] which are different in their nature and never to be confounded" (Shelley 348) was accepted as doctrine and is still a core belief in American Christianity today.

This idea fit perfectly into the new concept of Freedom. Freedom from Church persecution and from Church rule was only possible by the Grace of God Himself. It opened the door for the establishment and growth of dozens of brand new denominations.

Some lasted---some failed---but God had rewound His clock and set the alarm again. Before it would ring again and usher in the Second Great Awakening, we had some growing to do…A Revolutionary war; a Civil war; establish a solid government; and coming to some kind of agreement between the awkward conflict between Calvinism and Arminianism. This conflict actually defined the First and Second Great Awakening. The pendulum had swung from Calvinistic views way over to the extreme Arminianism side. A new movement was in the works.

IX.

THE SECOND GREAT AWAKENING

There is a huge difference between a movement and a denomination. A movement is an idea people gravitate toward. Those people bond into groups that eventually takes a name and becomes a denomination. All denominations are people who have rallied around a movement. Some movements attract millions of followers while others attract only a few. Remember, Christianity itself began in Judah as a denomination of Judaism and grew (under God's mighty hand) into its own religion, complete with its own denominations.

The Reformation, with all its grand ideas and freedoms, "unintentionally" shattered traditional Christendom. It prayed, preached, and fought for the truth until no single church remained, only what we now call denominations" (Shelley 34). This movement, called the Reformation, had fragmented the Church into groups. These groups---separated from one another by doctrinal beliefs---were the seeds of denominations. These seeds chartered and planted in American soil, nurtured by faith, freedom, and guarded by reason, sprouted during the First Great Awakening and begin to mature into the fruit-bearing plants during the Second Great Awakening.

"In sixteenth-century Europe only four major divisions separated Church doctrine: Lutheran, Reformed, Anabaptist, and Anglican" (Shelley 441). However, in America, the New World was settled---freedom of religion encouraged---the First Awakening woke people up---reason became the standard---and instead of looking to the east for Jesus' return, they found themselves looking west toward expansion. It was during this optimistic period that the Second Great Awakening really began.

The period (1791-1835) is the true source of American denominationalism as we know it today. Some seeds took root and grew strong while producing much fruit. Others dried up and vanished back into the rich soil from which they came. Still others gave a good run for prosperity but just couldn't stand on their own creeds. Moreover, all this time Europe was still crossing the pond with more new theologies and movements ready for transplantation into America's religious garden of democracy.

The fiery sermons of Edwards, Wesley, and Whitfield had not been forgotten. Revival was still in the air and by 1791, America had caught ablaze again! Something wonderful and spiritual was happening! With stability in doctrine exhibited by territorial denominationalism, revival was on the rise.

In the West, it was "camp meetings." These camp meetings often lasted for days and on the final day a mighty infusion of God's Spirit would fall upon the people and, as Stanford Murrell puts it, "the floor was soon crowded with the slain: their screams for mercy pierced even the heavens" (Murrell 146). The camp meetings caught on and swept the hearts and spirits of a nation! The power of God seemed to shake whole towns at a time. People came to the alter by the thousands.

In the east, the spirit of revival was stirred by dynamic personalities such as Charles Finney and George Williams. Finney, covering the east, led one of the most extensive evangelistic campaigns America had ever seen. Philadelphia, New York City, Rochester and other cities experienced the "new" method this man named Finney used to bring people to the Cross: praying for people by name; permitting women to pray and give personal testimonies; and a new thing called "an alter call!"

These new revival methods quickly became saturated with local social workers and reformers. One social worker named George Williams was so inspired by the lectures and reading of Finney that after conversion, in 1844 he was led to start a Christian based Community Club for boys. It's still with us today as the Y.M.C.A. (Murrell 148).

Despite the obvious good Finney accomplished, some pastors---conservatives mostly---accused him of changing American religion from a God-centered one to a man-centered one. Nevertheless, Finney was able to have a lasing influence on "future" Holiness and Pentecostal movements and leaders. Credited with the conversion of over 500,000 people, Finney's faithful followers spread and promoted his methods to the point where they are still standard in American Churches today.

A key factor to the evangelistic success of the Second Awakening as compared to the First was really evident in the Calvinistic verses Arminian approach to Biblical doctrine (see the chart below). The first Awakening was Calvinistic on the doctrine of predestined election (salvation only for those pre-selected by God), while the Second Awakening employed the Arminian concept of Salvation to all who simply believe and depend on God's love.

	First Great Awakening	Second Great Awakening

TIME FRAME	Early to mid-18th century	Early to mid-19th century
FORMATIVE ENVIRONMENT	Failure of Puritan theocracy	Frontier expansion
MAJOR FIGURES	Theodore J. Frelinghuysen William Tennent Gilbert Tennent Jonathan Edwards George Whitefield	Francis Asbury James McGready Barton Stone Peter Cartwright Charles G. Finney
MOST ACTIVE DENOMINATIONS	Dutch Reformed Presbyterian Congregational	Methodist Baptist
CHARACTERISTIC METHODS	Circuit riding Preaching in churches	Camp meetings Revivals in churches
THEOLOGY	Calvinist	Arminian
EMPHASIS	Doctrine	Experience
NEGATIVE SIDE EFFECTS	Unitarianism	American Cults

(From Walton's *Church History* p. 103)

It's a kind of a numbers game: the "everyone welcome" approach of the Arminian intrinsically appeals to more people than does the "only the elect' doctrine of Calvinism. The people listened with anxious ears and open hearts. This message is still a leading message today in even our most modern churches. "For God so loved the world…" (John 3:16) is the starting line. But Calvinism is still alive and strong as well. Both claim scriptural roots and divine guidance. This too is a hallmark of modern Christianity…the ability to tolerate opposing doctrinal views.

It's a debate from which we can't hide. No matter what church you belong to---even the so-called Non-Denominational ones--- you will be forced to decide one way or the other on the question: "Can you choose salvation yourself?" "And can you refuse election?"

A NOTE on Non-Denominational:

In spite of their name, yes, they are a "denomination." The very fact that they gather under a specific banner, that of "Non-Denominational," qualifies them as a denomination called "Non-Denominational." Not a traditional one, but a fast growing one.

FUNDAMENTALS TO FANATICS

To those who would believe, God laid out the foundation of His religion. He created it---He instructed men in how He wanted it practiced---and He gave it to us as a tool to be used to understand how to worship Him only. As mankind grew, (be fruitful and multiply) we eventually established governments, businesses, schools, sciences, and so on. In the process, we slowly turned our gaze away from God and onto ourselves. We began to use ourselves as the model to understanding God's ways. Rather than using God's Word as the measuring stick, we used ourselves as the example of "what's right."

Like Peter who walked on water as long as he kept focused on The Christ, and sank into the swirling sea when he looked away, man began to sink into the stormy seas of doubt and confusion when he turned his face away from the Creator. In essence, we forgot to look to God for His wisdom and for His guidance. As a result of this, we lost the full picture of God.

To illustrate this "drifting away," look at Adam: Adam was closer to God than any man in the history of humanity ever was. He physically walked and talked with God. In fact, before Woman was created from Adam's rib, he was an original, one-of-a-kind. He experienced God in ways we today can't even imagine.

Then like a Xerox machine, mankind began making copies of itself. Each human is a copy of those before him or her. Problem is that we are not perfect copies. We are flawed. We are copies of copies of copies. Each copy a tiny bit flawed from the one before us. Each generation is further from Adam's relationship to God than the one before it. Now, thousands of years later and thousands of copies later…copies of copies of copies…we are so far from the way God created us that we are almost another creature all together (read Romans 1:22-32 to discover what we really are).

To compensate for the copying-flaw, over the century's theologians (those who study God) came up with concepts they claim were lost in the copying process. Their presentation to civilization is really no different from the airbrush artist who touches up photographs for magazines. They are trying to juice it up a little: to fill in the empty spots, giving the illusion of guiding us back to God's original "religion of Himself."

However, there's a problem. We (theologians) are still using man's mind to reveal God's character and His ways. That's like an ant trying to imitate an elephant. It can't even come close. So regardless of intent, the theological concepts we come up with are flawed and become copies of copies for future generations to read. Each "new" theological idea we come up with impacts generations and their churches in general. The concepts of today can influence churches that aren't even built yet and effect people who aren't even born yet!

Some of these ideas are absorbed and incorporated as part of future belief systems, while other ideas fall away into just a memory. There are more of these theological ideas than I can list here, so I will keep it to a minimum and list the ones that had major impacts on the evolution of Christianity in America. These include Gnosticism, Deism, Socinianism, English Unitarianism, Lutheran Pietism, Foxes Quakers, the Moravians, Anglicans, Brethren movements and so on. I am going to add "slavery" (in America) to this section because both sides used Scripture to justify its own position.

As the nation grew, it also developed a robust thirst for new doctrine. Old books, forgotten theological works, and Pastor's journals were diligently recovered from dusty archives. Their pages cleaned up---edited---published---and presented to the public as the "latest find." Rehashing old works became the rage of the day.

Vast networks of "idea packaging" emerged and sold their wares as fact: as the *Lost Truths*: the *Lost Books*: and the *Rediscovered Mysteries*. American Christianity was thrust into a doctrinal feeding frenzy! Old ideas became fads. Fads became movements. Movements became doctrine: and these doctrines were (and still are) incorporated into churches which themselves became new denominations. They split and split again…becoming copies of copies of copies…different from the original. So different, in fact, that they even had to come up with new names. These new denominations, these copies of copies, became bricks on which the road to modern American Christianity is to be paved. The blocks of rehashed theological concepts became the building blocks while religious diversity became the mortar that supported them as well as separated them.

Through this process, we became a nation of Fundamentalist and Fanatics. A mix and match people with a pick and choose attitude about everything. Pick a *Bible* translation you like---match it to a denomination you feel comfortable with---choose which doctrine you agree with---make all the decisions yourself as long as you feel "good"---then sit back and enjoy the security of knowing your place in the Kingdom is secure. The motto is, "If you don't like it…be bold…step out…change it!"

Yes, we've come a long way from the Christianity the Christ started along the dusty roads of Judea. Let's take a brief look at some of the more popular theological concepts that found fertile ground in American Christianity. Each has become an ingredient in our Great *Denominational Stew*.

GNOSTICISM

It's been around for a long, long time. The basic teaching

of Gnostics (*"gnosis"* meaning "knowledge") was that "matter is essentially evil and spirit is essentially good." They teach the "Clockwork Universe" *thermo*: like a master clockmaker, God created the universe, wound it up and stepped back to let it run down. Our only way to know God who is entirely good, therefore totally spirit, is through reading the *Bible* as all-spiritual. For example, since God made man in His image (Genesis 1:27) and He created both male and female, then it only makes sense that God is both male as well as female. This type of reasoning is Gnosticism at its finest! (For more on this see John McArthur's book, *Truth Wars*, p. 91-92).

Gnosticism is ancient, reaching back to the days of the Apostles and even further. Its special brand of spiritual over reasoning found fertile ground in the ideologies of the American public. The Age of Reason picked it up and ran with it! The Quakers "Inner Light," the Swendenborge communication with the dead, and even the so-called "white magic" of delusional Wiccans today depend on spirit guides to discover hidden truths and powers reserved for only those willing to seek it out. The Mysticism…this Gnostic magic and spiritualism by any other name…is actually rebellion against God. Rather than depending on the Father in prayer and in faith, Gnosticism teaches that by speaking in a magical (secret) language---even a single word or phrase---one can reach the spirit world (which is all "good") and actually control it…make it bend to our will. This is the stuff cults are made of today. It has been around a long time and doesn't look like its going to go away any day soon. (See Word Faith Movement in INDEX).

DEISM (1583-1648)

Deism (Latin for *"dues,"* which is "God") primarily emerged from the writings of Lord Herbett Cherbury (1583-1648) as an important rationalistic movement in England before being embraced in the American colonies as well (Murrell 125). Deist, such as our Benjamin Franklin, argued that like the Gnostics the universe functions on its own, therefore (logically) miracles are to be denied and concepts such as the atoning work of Christ and the regenerating work of the Holy Spirit are to be rejected. The Bible is not unique and the supernatural is merely superstition. The light is the light of nature (natural laws) and man must observe and rely on his own reason.

NOTE: Although not Deistic, Wicca---Americanized Witchcraft---often called "the Old Religion"---teaches that the way to spiritual control is through understanding nature (Mother Earth) and "discovering" the power hidden in it. Once discovered, these 'secrets" are written down in sacred books and passed down from generation to generation to assist Wicca *descendants* to better control the spiritual. It's Deism with a twist!

Through the writings of Cherbury (the Father of Deism), the Deistic movement took on an air of religion. They used the format of Christianity as grounds for unified and ethical behavior, but put man's reason in charge of laws and daily life. For example, when Benjamin Franklin said that "Honesty if the best policy," he meant that people should be honest because it's practical to be honest. It pays to be honest. It's civilized and compatible with reason. This thinking is far different from the concept that people should be honest because the Creator instructed us to be honest…to live in an honest manner.

The desire to live a good life can easily give the illusion that one is living a godly life. To the Deist there is no such distinction. God made us in His image, so whatever we do as long as we don't hurt anyone else, is godly and good. Deists are masters of justification… just what a budding country needed when confronted with uncomfortable questions about sin. This is dangerous ground and is rooted in the crippling sin of pride. Pride of life (1 John 2:15-16) is a blindly serious sin…it is so easy to justify our behavior, to justify what we want…that it can destroy our life as we are proudly staring in the mirror admiring all we have.

SOCINIANISM

"Two Roman Catholics, Laelius Socinus and his nephew, Faustus Sociuns (1539-1604) were responsible for promoting doctrinal error that denied cardinal truths held by the RCC "(Murrell 116). They didn't outright attack the Church but, like Satan questioning the Woman in the Garden, they raised clever questions that raised even more questions. (Paul warned us about these types of people in II Timothy 2:3 and 3:5...he said to "avoid them").

Finally, in Poland in 1605 the nephew put it all together and published his work as the *"Rocovian Catechism."* In it, the deity of Christ is denied. Jesus was declared a good man, but still only a man (much like Islam teaches today). His death at Calvary did not atone for our sins and the Bible could be changed---updated---as civilization demanded. The followers of Socinus were not out to destroy Christianity but in their zeal to break down the Catholic empire they crucified Christ all over again. This time as just a man. They were so filled with defiance that on the tomb of their leader they inscribed, "Lofty Babylon lies prostrate. Luther destroyed its rod, Calvin its walls, but Socinus its foundations" (Murrell 116).

The Catholic Church was the enemy of the Socianians so they built a theology, which, out of defiance, stood against the things the Church had stood for. This is important because hate is not easily extinguishable. It tends to come back in other forms. Much like the Seventh Day Adventist bitterness for the Catholic Church is so great that they tend to twist scripture drastically to "prove" that she is the Beast of Revelation 13. Hate is a terrible thing. It blinds us from truth and leads us to take false trails.

UNITARIANISM (1774)

Those in England who embraced Socinianism were known as "Unitarians." They held that Scripture was open to personal interpretation. In 1774, some 40 ministers pulled away from the

Episcopal Church (also known as the Church of England) to form a Unitarian Church in London. (Later to reach America as the Unitarian Universalist Church).

They held that God is a solitary entity (No Trinity) and has revealed himself through various men and books: Buddha's, Mohammed, Confucius, Lao and others are all sources of revelation, none of which stands alone. Early in the history of America the Unitarian faith was revealed through the work of preachers such as Jonathan Mayhew (1720-1766), Joseph Priestly (1794), Hosey Ballou (1771-1852), and even poets such as Ralph Waldo Emerson in 1838 (Martin 502).

Although they deny the deity of Jesus as God and part of the Trinity, they accept His teachings on spiritualism and good moral living. They deny the traditional ideas of a Heaven and a Hell relying more on the deity of man as we make ourselves into "our" idea of a god. Therefore, if one is to pattern his or her life after Christ, they are Christians in morality only. This "made in our image" philosophy became ingrained in the American image of itself. "We're right and everyone else is wrong: or is a savage: or is in the way or our progress." A religious kind of ethocentristic mind-set. This belief is still with us today and has a powerful grip on our way of viewing our nation's role in world affairs. (See INDEX for more on this).

LUTHERAN PIETISM (1670)

"Mysticism came to the Lutheran Church in the seventeenth century in the form of Pietism" (Murrell 111). It would later cross-political boundaries to influence many orders of Christendom, including the Puritans. Pietism emphasized the need for a personal work-regeneration followed by a life of constant Christian living, private study of the Bible and home study groups. They avoided formal titles and introduced nouns such as "brother, sister," and even "pastor" as terms of address (Murrell 111).

The celebrated father of Pietism was the German born Phillip

Jacob Spener (1635-1705). He believed there was more to Christian life than remembering catechisms and attending Church on Sundays. Open drunkenness and immorality was so commonplace that no one seemed to even notice it as sin. He, to put it in simple terms, promoted Christian ethics as the way of life.

This, of course, was open to extremism. Just as the uppity-attitude of some disgruntled Puritans of the day is legendary and even become self destructive as displayed in the Salem Witch trials of 1693. Nevertheless, this ethocenristic behavior has become a major player in American characteristics. It has flowed over into our work places, our homes, and even our sports. We are an adversarial nation verging on the extreme side of arrogance. There is nothing categorically wrong with pietism as long as one remembers to honor God in humbleness and humility first.

To close out this section on Pietism: "If you are given a gold metal for humility…could you wear it?" A Lutheran Piests would proudly wear it, whereas a humble person couldn't bring himself to wear it. I once heard a televangelist make a Piest statement on TV. He said, "God had blessed me so much that I don't have a single suit that cost less than one-thousand dollars!" Piest, yes. Humble, no. The modern statement that reflects this Piests attitude is still with us is the comment, "Holier than thou." It is meant to point out how the person thinks he or she is exactly that: "they think they are holier than others." (This is part of the America attitude today).

FOXES QUAKERS (1654)

A man by the name of George Fox (1624-1691) introduced new behavior for Christians to practice. A deeply religious man, Fox stressed sincerity in religion and a spiritual visitation from God. He believed that men possessed what he called the "Inner Light." This is our guide to right and wrong---to false and true---to low and high---and between pure to impure.

Christ's light is the divine illumination that gives life and power and peace and joy. One's goal is to merge our Inner light with Christ's Light. This is accomplished through spiritual living, security in faith, and replaying scripture "within" until it becomes manifested in one's outer-self through works and actions. Good works and "shaking and quaking" (much like today's Pentecostals speaking in tongues) as an outer sign to reveal an inner happening.

In 1654, there were only 60 Quakers. Four years later there were thirty thousand! The origin of the name "Quaker" is uncertain, but tradition has it that Fox, who had been called before the court for blasphemy charges advised the judge that "It was he (the judge) who should 'trimble and quake' at the Word of God." The name stuck, but Fox preferred his followers to be called "Friends" after John 15:15, "I have called you friends… (For more on Fox, see INDEX).

Doctrinally, they stress the priesthood of all believers. They did not take any oaths, go to war, or retaliate when persecuted. In Church, they would sit in silence waiting for the Spirit to stir someone to speak. If none felt "moved" to speak they left and went home---assured that all was in order.

This feeling of "being moved to speak" or to "act out" in some way when one feels the presence of God (or the Holy Ghost) is still a part of many American Denominations of Christianity today… especially in the Charismatic movements and Churches.

MORAVIANS (1727)

Out of the Unity of the Brethren movement during the days of Martin Luther, the Bohemian Brethren counted membership at 200,000 but during the Thirty-Year-War, it was almost destroyed. (The survivors were later referred to as the "Hidden Seeds"). In 1720, a young Lutheran named Nikolous Ludwig Von Zinzendorf emerged to revive them. He began with just two families and in just five-short-years, several hundred Brethren had gathered. The people were forced-moved to the Providence of Moravian where they adopted the name of "Moravians."

Officially, the Moravian Church was opened in 1737 and demonstrated the presence of the Holy Spirit in a special way. Zinzendorf taught believers to be faithful and to conquer the nations of the world by making Disciples of them based on Matthew 28:19-29. Missionaries were dispatched to Africa, Asia, Greenland, and North America. This group of Disciples fanned the flames of Protestant missionary work. It is still with us today...almost exclusively American now. (For more, see INDEX).

When families moved to America in 1740, they settled along the Delaware River. There they faithfully worked with the Indians and poorer German settlers scattered in Pennsylvania. In 1741, Count Zinzendorf visited the colony and on Christmas Eve naming it, "Bethlehem" (House of Bread) in a symbolic gesture of all who hunger can come to this colony and find the Living Bread of Jesus. This missionary zeal is still a major part of American Christianity today. Spreading the Gospel has become almost exclusively the work of American Missionaries and a major taste in our *Stew*. It's like adding Charity as a flavoring!

ANGLICANS

Anglicans are traced to the Church of England (As already covered in Part IV, Reformation & Royalty). Henry VIII outlawed Catholicism in England in 1534 and took the Churches for the State. He declared himself Head of the Churches and renamed them the "Church of England." This sparked decades of religious divergence. Each succeeding Monarch changed the rules of worship according to their own personal or political views.

Out of this came Congregationalist, Separatist, Puritans and so on. It became so strained at times that King Charles, the son of King James I, promoted the "Divine Right of Kings" (Murrell 87) and disbanded even Parliament in 1640. He and he alone, would rule the land and its Churches: the Church of England and its Anglican members. It became known as the "Anglican Church" in title but was physically the old Catholic Churches buildings, most of its tradition, ritual, and teachings. It was difficult sometimes to even distinguish an Anglican Priest from a Catholic one. It had all the trappings of the Catholic Church but no Pope. The King took that position for himself, by a different title of course.

Over time, the Anglican Church came to America in the early 1700's and took the name of Episcopal. With England backing it in the New Land, it was established as the Official Church of the Americas. The Puritans wouldn't hear of it! Although it was not the R.C.C., it was the R.C.C. made over and empowered by the State. For this reason the Episcopal Church (Anglican) never caught on as strongly as English Monarchs had hoped it would, but its seed is still with us today: still struggling to get a political foothold in America.

Americans still have the heart of the nation's Puritan founders and even now shy away from anything that hints of a wolf-in-political-clothing (See Matthew 7:15). This caution against "Official" churches is a part of our Great *Stew*…a part that keeps it vibrant and from turning sour.

PLYMOUTH BRETHREN (1827)

"Another group which emerged during the time of reaction against the sterility of the Anglican Church was the Brethren" (Murrell 129). In 1826, an Anglican Priest, John Darby, in South London, began holding home worship services. Out of these gatherings came camaraderie and a sense of unity: of brotherhood. The Brethren Movement was founded!

They believed that since every believer is a priest (see Revelation 1:6 and 1 Peter 2:9) there should be no ordained ministers. All creeds were opposed and worship should be conducted according to the Apostle's example. All formalism and traditions were rejected and all doctrine needed to be re-evaluated. As Brethren grew so did their doctrinal distinctive.

Darby (and later Edward Irving) introduced to the Christian community concepts that had never before been considered by the Church in its eighteen hundred years of existence (Murrell 130). After a riding accident in 1827, Darby formulated new views of eschatology (end time studies). Darby's belief was a pre-millennial interpretation of the end times. He claimed that the collective eschatology of the Church had been wrong for almost two-thousand-years. He was the first to teach that "at the rapture Jesus will turn around and go back to Heaven---then come again after our time of tribulation." He called the rapture the "First Advent," and the "Second Advent" signaled the start of the thousand-year reign of Christ. The idea that men are allowed to re-analogize end time teaching and promote their own personal beliefs is a hallmark of American Christianity even today.

This Brethren Church concept is alive and well in home Bible groups; in outside Church activities; in Christian movies and books; and in almost every outside "the Church house" meetings. All one needs is an open mind and a crowd that is willing to listen.

SPIRITUALISM

"Mysticism" by another name, Spiritualism has been around since the beginning of recorded history. It is simply a metaphysical way of viewing cause and effect relationships in our world. It attempts to explain how the unseen world affects the seen world. In its extreme, Spiritualism encompasses mysticism, channeling, psychic surgery, astral projection, witchcraft (to an extent), superstition, and myth building.

The colonial settlers who were fleeing Europe's Inquisitional Witch hunts were well aware of the dangers of Spiritualism in itself, so they shunned it and all connections with it as evil. Even America's one and only period of witch trials (Salem) only lasted slightly little more than one year (1692-1693).

Then around 1862 a frail woman in ill health named, Mary Baker

Eddy, burst onto the scene with her spiritual healing methods. She opened Churches, wrote books, started a publishing company and (like Gloria Copeland today) started a Healing School for Christians. She ordained her organization a denomination and titled it "Church of Christian Scientist (Funk & Wagnall's vol. 9, p. 38). Then in 1881, she landed her Mother Church in Boston along with her prize: "the Massachusetts Metaphysical College." The college, along with her self-promoting publishing company, spread her personal brand of Christianity and Spiritualism. (For more on Eddy see INDEX).

Mary Baker Eddy was not the first or only spiritualist to influence American Christianity, but she is the most well known and can be viewed as the standard by which others aspire to follow. It is a very dangerous thing to place "spiritualism before salvation" as the message of Jesus. Those who do usually end up promoting psychic healings, channeling, white magic, and even use cults who claim "God is driving a flying saucer" as witness to their message.

This type of message is so common today that it easily blends in un-noticed and leads people, especially the young and inexperienced, to feel comfortable with its dangers. They mistakenly think that if it has the name of "Jesus" in it somewhere then it must be ok to explore and try to use. How wrong they are! It is the sin of Balaam all over again. This is the extra spicy part of our *Stew*...it gives it an exotic flavor...unhealthy, but some like it that way.

SLAVERY (1865)

Slavery has been somewhat of an anomaly in America if we are to promote Christian love and unity. The prime example is that of Thomas Jefferson. How could he write, "all men are created equal," while at the same time he was a slave owner himself (Murrell 145)?

Many arguments---both for and against this "peculiar institution"---have been made. The Patriarch Abraham was cited as having slaves, as well as the Book of Philemon was used to flavor slavery as "ok." It got pretty wild with the other side quoting that enslaving another human is violating Jesus' command to do unto others as you would have them do unto you, as well as 1 Timothy 1:10 condemning slavers (as "man stealers")... Remember, as discussed throughout Section One everyone is a product of his or her time. Colonial America---even throughout the Civil War days--- were men of their time. Even by constructing the 13th Amendment (ratified 1865), the issue of slavery would not be easily erased. The Civil War left a gaping wound in the body of Christ in America. This wound would not be so easy to heal. It will take a lot of time and understanding on both sides.

Christians, American Christians, split often and killed one another over this issue! (Killing in the name of God again?). New denominations were often formed after splits with established groups. Christians in the South who defended the literal words of the *Bible* insisted on a strict and narrow interpretation. Those in the North who opposed slavery emphasized the spiritual and ethical principles of the *Bible*. Sadly, even today, the effect of the Civil War, death, and racial intolerance brings out the worst in people.

Christians would split on the Civil Right issues and many Christians were divided by race. However, with the West fully opened up and settled and slavery finally outlawed in the Land of Freedom, America got back to the business of building a future for its flock and to figuring out the correct way to make our *Stew*.

SHAMANISM

Shamanism is the belief, similar to Witchcraft and Spiritualism, where the Shaman is believed to be endowed with certain psychic abilities that allow him or her to communicate with the spirit world (Mead 304). This belief is prevalent in most primitive cultures including the African Bushmen, the Australian Aborigines, Voo Doo priest and Native American Indians. (See Native American Church in INDEX). It has embedded itself in contemporary America as part of the "Back to Nature" movements.

In some Shamanistic Native American traditions their religion is popularly, but inaccurately, called a "peyote religion" because ceremonies frequently make use of a hallucinogenic plant of the cactus family: peyote" (Mead 303). The ritualistic use of this drug sparked a tidal wave of interest from the New Agers (see New Age in INDEX) who used marijuana and other drugs for a "spiritual high." All of a sudden, everyone and their dog were claiming to be Native American.

Hollywood began churning out film after film glamorizing shamanistic rituals. The peace pipe, sweat lodge, vision quest, and peyote were popularized by movies such as *Billy Jack, Little Big Man*, and *A man Called Horse*. Out of this came a landslide of New-Age Shamanistic literature. One especially popular book titled *Black Elk Speaks*, by John Neihard, was updated from its 1932 edition and quickly became a major guidebook for New Agers (mostly white) who were seeking to re-connect with nature.

These seekers were searching for guidance into any nature-based mysticism in which "Mother Earth" and all her inhabitants could live in ecological and spiritual harmony. The idea of having a Shaman to guide them was appealing and was quickly absorbed into American culture as part of the 60's "back to nature" ideas.

An example of just how far this Shamanistic concept of contacting the spirit-world through hallucinogenic and psychic leaders has reached, the following article from a respected Christian Magazine titled, "*The Berean Call*," demonstrates how it is practiced by some in the highest seats of influence in our nation's capital:

> Hillary Clinton has long promoted shamanism, including public endorsements. Placing her on its front cover with the caption "The Most Powerful Woman," *Time Magazine* declared, "Just by her being herself, Hillary Rodham Clinton has redefined the role of First Lady." Inside was a picture of this "most

powerful woman" [who claims to be a Christian] being blessed by a Native American spiritual healer: a Shaman. (Hunt 8)

Such practices have saturated the American belief to the point of open acceptance. Shamanistic principles are virtually undistinguishable from Wicca, the Brujas of Mexico, and even the Voo Doo priest of Haiti. All the way from the beggar on the streets to the steps of the White House itself, Shamanism has been endorsed through public opinion. Once again, man has put God's Word aside in favor of public opinion of what's cool and acceptable. (See INDEX for more on New Age).

Like so many other movements and belief systems already mentioned, Shamanistic Mysticism and its ideas about the spirit-world has been synthesized into American Christian Denominations in subtle ways. It is now a major part of our *Stew*. It gives it that exotic-mystical flavor! However, like most spicy foods, watch out for the coming heartburn.

XI.

<u>TO EACH HIS OWN</u>

By the 1900's America was armed and ready for a denominational explosion, and like most exploding bombs, fragments and shrapnel flew in every direction. Some fragments wounded the nation--- some went un-noticed—while others actually helped it to grow spiritually. On the religious front established denominations tightened and enforced their doctrinal views while members who didn't agree pulled away and formed their own groups...soon to become new denominations, sub-denominations, or the unheard of American phenomenon of "non-denominational."

With all this flood of theological components: "Gnosticism, Deism, Unitarianism, Spiritualism and so on," one could simply pick-n-choose…mix-and–match…or create your own unique "brand" of worship. Of course, each group claimed to be the correct way and all the others were well intended but off the mark. This "correct way" idea wasn't confined to religion alone but was evenly spread across the board of American culture. We were on the forefront of new advances…of big changes…changes in all areas of life. Changes in physics, philosophy, art, economics, and government, all contributed to our new ways of adapting to change. For example:

--- In 1905 Albert Einstein published his *Special Theory of Relativity* (a new way of thinking about time and space).

--- In 1926 Schrodinger developed Quantum mechanics (a new way to think about tiny particles).

--- In 1945 the USA exploded its first atomic bomb (a new way of thinking about weapons of war).

---Karl Marx wrote his *Communist Manifesto* (a new way to think about labor).

---Friedrich Nietzsche preached his ideas on man's desire for personal power and human superiority.

---The existentialists such as Jean Paul Sartre and Albert Camus gave new insights into man's nothingness and total powerlessness over the ages.

---Art seemed to join the marathon as it raced from Neoclassic to Impressionists. From Expressionism to Surrealism and from Modern and Pop into Absurd and Minimalism.

---Music changed in similar leaps and bounds, but nothing compared to the changes in economics.

In economics the European concept of Capitalism had matured on American shores and was actually competing with Christianity as the motivating force in daily life. American Capitalism had performed not just well, but brilliantly! "Despite our submerged one-fourth of a nation, we were closer than any community in history in attaining the bright goal of being an economy without poverty" (Heilbroner 256). In an attempt to justify our drive for wealth we even had "IN GOD WE TRUST" imprinted on our US coins…making each coin a magic amulet!

All these ideas came together in the land of freedom to make us what we are today. Laws were created---changed---added to and amended. Somehow in the mix the idea of "One Nation Under God" remained strong and guided our nation toward a blazing future. We seemed to have it all: wealth, power, a modular pick-n-choose religion. Were we truly the "city on the hill?" Or were we simply a flash in the pan?

Is our future a God ordained future? A chaotic future? Will our *Denominational Stew* burn up---boil over---or feed the world with the Bread of Life? The next Section, "Contemporary America," will show the current results of Denominationalism in this land of, "to each his own," by showing today's denominations as single units of a whole country.

PART THREE
Contemporary America

XII.

DENOMINATIONS AS INDIVIDUAL UNITS

It was assumed, until modern times, that civic harmony depended upon religious conformity. Religion influenced law; law governed people; and multitudes of people made up the One Country. King Louis XIV reflected this in is famous statement: "One King, one faith, one law" (Mead). Social conformity is necessary for stability and growth and America took it one-step further with its **"E PLURBUS UNUM"** (out of many, one) concept of unity through diversity. Does this hold true for Christianity as well? Can it survive in its many denominational parts?

The Apostle Paul, in I Corinthians 12:13 tells us that: "For as the body is one [*Unum*] and hath many members [*Pluribus*] and all the members of that one body, being many, are one body…" Therefore, if we can withhold our judgments and personal convictions and look at all current Christian Denominations as the many parts of One Body, we can begin to get a grip on American Denominationalism.

There are literally hundreds of different denominations (parts of the body) in America today. In addition, if we count the "non-denominations" it would reach well into the thousands! Some parts of the body of Christianity are scripturally healthy while others are weak, sickly, and cancerous. Some are functioning at maximum glory while others barely function at all. However, like it or not, all play a part in the overall body of American Christianity.

Of course, we can't look at all of them in this book, so we'll look at the major ones. The ones that have established roots in freedom's soil and influence us today.

In this Section, "Contemporary America," I will try to present the major denominations in a fair, factual and non-judgmental manner: where each comes from; their journey to where they are today; and what they practice, believe, and how they differ from others. I realize that no paper can satisfy everyone because we are all ethnocentristic by nature. Some may feel cheated because I did not devote the time or space they think a particular person, event, or denomination deserves.

Remember, this is NOT a recruiting tool. It's meant only as a general history and information on denominations and how each fits into contemporary American lifestyle. It's not like trying to unscramble an egg. This is a *Stew*. It's made up of individual, traceable pieces with written history to investigate from which we can learn. Each piece is distinguishable from the others and its these pieces that audaciously make up the many denominations we have today.

In order to obtain reliable first-hand information to help us identify these individual chunks in our *Stew* I mailed out Survey Letters to different denominational headquarters throughout America. Most who responded also sent their denominational literature along with their responses. This section is the result of these first-hand survey letters, denominational literature, accepted reference books on denominations, and various encyclopedias.

In order not to give any single group preeminence or the illusion of superior importance over another, I will simply list them in alphabetical order. The Great *American Denominational Stew* is hot and ready to serve. Ring the dinner bell…

ADVENTIST (Seventh Day)

"Throughout the history of Christianity there have been communities and individuals who have awaited the return or Jesus Christ [the Advent] with eager anticipation" (Mead 256). This eagerly awaiting the Advent is universal in Christianity, but the movement that has been termed "Adventist" is a purely American product. The Adventist Church is a fruit of American Freedom and ideology. Even the term "New World" conjures up images of the millennial kingdom: the time was right for Christ' coming kingdom!

The Adventist family of Churches was born in the era of great hopes: of looking toward the future---eternal hope. Today they are regarded as conservative Protestants with the Seventh Day Adventist Church being the largest branch and most representatives of Adventist thought and practice. An old-school name for this line of thought is "the Millerite Movement," named for the post-revolutionary Baptist-turned-Deist, William Miller. William Miller (1782-1849) was born in Pittsfield, Massachusetts in 1782. He was a farmer, a regular Baptist and a respected soldier in the War of 1812. Later he converted to Deism, which teaches that although God did create the world out of nothing, He is now uninvolved and governs it only through unchangeable eternal laws. The term "clockwork universe" is often used to illustrate this concept. (See Deism in INDEX for more).

"During the Second Great Awakening (1816) Miller experienced a powerful conversion back to traditional Christianity. He became a fervent student of the Bible, with special interest in the books of Daniel and Revelation" (Rhodes 21). Following the chronology espoused by Bishop Ussher who dated the creation of the world at 4004 B.C., Miller concluded (in 1818) that Christ' Second Coming could also be calculated from the Bible. He found his proof in the so-called "seventy-weeks of Daniel" and in the 2,300 days of Daniel 9:24, among others.

Miller concluded that the return of Jesus (the "cleansing") would occur between March 21, 1843 and March 21, 1844 (Martin 411-12). He lectured on this and gathered a large following. These followers were labeled, "Millerites," and at the specified time anxiously awaited the second coming---"the Advent of Jesus Christ." "There were between fifty and one-hundred thousand people in the United States awaiting the great day" (Mead 258).

When it turned out to be a false alarm Miller and his associates reassessed his calculations and arrived at a new Advent date: "October 22, 1844." This too proved a disappointment. In Advent literature, this is referred to as "the Great Disappointment." Because of this let down, many gave up on Adventism and many gave up on the Christian faith itself...yet others still retained Miller's basic idea and continued the search for a better date.

These searchers---these survivors of the Great Disappointment---came together in April of 1845 in Albany, New York to define and to order their common beliefs. They agreed on the following:

1) The world will be totally destroyed by fire and a new one will be created.

2) There will be two Advents of Christ; both will be visible.

3) Conditions for participating in the millennial reign of Christ are faith, good works and living a Godly life.

4) There will be two resurrections: the resurrection of the believers at Christ' return and the resurrection of unbelievers after the millennial reign (the Great White Throne Judgment).

Despite earnest efforts to come together, they still disagreed over issues:

1) Do the lost suffer eternally in Hell, or are they immediately/eternally destroyed?

2) Are the dead conscious our unconscious?

3) Is the Sabbath on the first day of the week (Sunday) or is it on the seventh day of the week (Saturday)?

"Controversies over these issues gave rise to a variety of Adventist groups" (Rhodes). These groups, for the most part, agreed that Miller had indeed been wrong on some points but not wrong about the date being important. Something happened on that date (1844) of great importance. A well-respected teacher named Hiram Edson (1806-92) claimed that on that date the ministry of Christ had moved from the Holy into the Most Holy Place for the "investigative judgment.' The hour of judgment had come! This is called the "Doctrine of the Sanctuary."

Next, the issue of the Sabbath day was settled by Joseph Bates (1792-1872) who showed through scripture that the proper way to uphold God's 4th commandment was to keep Saturday as the Holy Sabbath. Then a third group from the state of Maine emphasized the "Doctrine of the Spirit of Prophecy." They showed how in the last days the Spirit would be manifest in the remnant, or last segment, of God's True Church. "These three doctrines [teachings] came together to form what was called the Seventh Day Adventist Church (Martin 415).

The embodiment of the third part (the Spirit of Prophesy) was found in a dynamic woman, Ellen G. White (1823-1925). Without going into E. G. White's long and colorful history it will suffice to say that she was believed to be a modern-day Prophet, was well respected, a savvy business person, a noted author, and is popularly recognized as the founder of the Seventh Day Adventist Church as it is today. Two of her many books, *"The Great Controversy,"* and *"Desire of the Heart,"* are still quoted today in scholarly Adventist circles.

By holding to the writings of E. G. White and by adhering to the three core teachings (the Investigative Judgment, the Second Advent, and the Spirit of Prophecy) the church grew at record-breaking speed. Although some classified the S.D.A. as a cult, many have changed their opinion and welcomed them into mainline Christianity. For example, Walter Martin, the author of the respected text, *"Kingdom of the Cults"* is one who retracted his old-cult label... see pages 409-411 of his book.

Beliefs & Practices

As for modern Adventist, most describe the S.D.A. Church as Adventist in belief---Protestant in tradition---Orthodox in practice---and Conservative in presentation and dress. Some of their doctrine and practices are:

> ---The Bible (prefer the KJV) is the infallible expression of God's will:

> ---There is one God in three persons (Father, Son, and Holy Ghost):

> ---Jesus lived a sinless life, died on the cross, rose from the dead and ascended to Heaven where He administers judgment today:

> ---The Holy Spirit gives spiritual gifts to equip believers for the ministry:

> ---The S.D.A. focuses primarily on the gift of prophecy and questions the authenticity of claims of speaking in tongues:

> ---Salvation is by grace, and obedience to the Commands is the fruits of salvation:

> ---Saturday is the correct day of worship, and keeping

Sunday as the Sabbath is the "sign of the Beast" and his church:

---Church government is presbyterial:

---Women cannot be ordained:

---Baptism is by immersion and only for those mature enough to confess Christ as their Savior:

---The Lord's Supper is practiced "in remembrance" and foot washing is often practiced before the supper is attended:

---The lost will be destroyed in the Lake of Fire rather than suffer for eternity:

---The S.D.A. advocates complete separation of Church and State:

---They have over fifty publishing houses around the world and promote private as well as public education with 90 colleges around the globe. They are very active in nearly every country:

---They are very active in foreign missions and operate 7,000 weekly radio and television broadcast in nearly every county:

---They hold as close as possibly to the clean and unclean food standards of Levitical Law, especially the "no pork" rules:

---Lastly, unlike some denominations who inflate their membership rolls by counting children and infants as "members," the S.D.A. only counts those actually baptized on membership rolls (Mead 272-73).

Born out of the "Great Disappointment" into the "Great Hope" of the second coming of Christ, the S.D.A. has become a sweet-and-sour flavor in our *Great American Denominational Stew*. Their passion for Christ---their love of the Bible---and their faith in God's promises have given them a solid place in this land from which our *Denominational Stew* is formed.

BAPTIST

Baptist consists of one of the largest and most diverse groups of Christians in the United States. Baptist are divided into around 27 different sub-denominations, the (Southern Baptist Convention being the largest) and makeup around one-third to one-half of the entire Protestant population in the USA (Funk & Wagnall vol. 3, p 269). Although they have never adopted a universal creed, the large membership alone unites them, giving the Baptist Church tremendous political strength in elections. The Baptist Church is an excellent example of "separate yet united" in modern American society.

The history of the Baptist Church is as varied as their individual beliefs. Even Baptist Scholars cannot come to full agreement regarding exact Baptist origins. According to Ron R. Rhodes, author of *"The Complete Guide to Christian Denominations,"* there are three theories about the origin of the Baptist Church:

1. The Jerusalem-Jordan-John Theory is a common view among Landmark Baptist. They hold that Baptist have existed since the days of John the Baptizer's ministry along the Jordan River. This would have the Baptist Church predating Protestantism and all other Christian denominations (including the R.C.C.). Problem is that there is no historical support for this line of descent. All churches have some similarities to the first-century Church.

2. The Anabaptist Spiritual Kingship Theory seeks to trace a spiritual relationship with modern Baptist from a long line of Anabaptist sects---including Swiss Anabaptist, Waldensians,

Petrobusians, Henricians, and so on up to modern day Baptist Churches. The problem with this theory is that Baptist have a long disagreed with key theological positions held by the Anabaptist. Positions such as swearing of oaths, holding public office, pacifism, modest dress, and soul sleep. This makes any direct lineage from the Anabaptist to modern Baptist unlikely except in name only.

3. The Separatist Descent Theory claims that the modern Baptist Church emerged out of 12th century English Separatist who believed baptism was to be reserved for adults only. The theology of early Baptist supports this theory. Under this model, the first Baptist Church of historical record was in Amsterdam in 1609 and "the first English baptism was conducted in 1611…the same year the King James Bible was produced" (Rhodes 35-36).

The first English Baptist Church was founded under the leadership of a Congregational Separatist, John Smith (1570-1612). It was Armenian in theology, emphasizing that Christ died for all people. These early Baptist were called "General Baptist" due to their belief that salvation was "generally" available to all. Later, in the 1630's Calvinistic Baptist Churches emerged in England teaching that salvation was limited to particular individuals only [the elect] so they were called "Particular Baptist" (Rhodes 35-36). "Eventually these two groups [General and Particular] united in the 19th century when theological issues had changed and the need of an effective missionary advance drew them together" (Funk & Wagnall vol. 3, p 270).

In Europe, the Baptist Church continued to grow into the tens-of-thousands but it was in America where it experienced its greatest growth. A Puritan clergyman named Roger Williams founded America's first Baptist Church at Providence, Rhode Island. One year later a minister (who later became a physician) named John Clard established a Baptist congregation at Newport, Rhode Island. The Baptist idea became popular by becoming ardent supporters of the American Revolution.

Even though the Baptist were never uniformly in agreement on all issues, by 1895 they had become a major force in America's economics, politics, educational systems, and ideas about State and Religion. Interestingly, even though various Baptist Churches have different theological and doctrinal beliefs…there is still a certain flavor…a certain air of unity about them as a whole. They have different ideas about their origins and practices but the doctrine of "the believer's baptism by immersion" comes forth as a consistent belief among them all.

Baptist not only reject the practice of infant baptism but proclaim that baptism by immersion rather than by pouring (offusion) or sprinkling (affusion) best follows the example of Jesus' own baptism in the river Jordan. They teach that it corresponds symbolically with the death and resurrection of Jesus as well as the Pauline symbolism of death of the "Old Self" and "putting on of the new man" (Ephesians 4:24). They never teach that baptism itself saves or is the invitation for the Holy Ghost to enter into the believer. They teach that these events already took place at the moment of true conversion.

Beliefs & Practices

---Baptist, for the most, agree on eternal security: that after conversion you cannot loose or surrender your God given salvation:

---They teach the total Holiness and Absolute Sovereignty of God: the oneness of God (Trinity) that God is one yet three persons…"God the Father, God the Son, and God the Holy Spirit:"

---In some Baptist Churches no one who has been divorced can hold a leadership position (this later became a huge source of Pastors for non-denominational Churches):

---Tithing, church membership, evangelism, missions, instrumental as well as vocal music is encouraged while most other issues including speaking in tongues, healing by faith and communion procedures are left open to individual congregations.

NOTE on early Black Baptist Churches in America: Usually slaves sat in the galleries of white churches, identifying with the faith of their owners but slowly this changed. The first Black Baptist Church was organized at Silver Bluff near Augusta, Georgia in 1773. By 1793, there were only 73,478 Baptist in the United States…and one fourth of them were blacks.

The Slave Rebellion, led by Nat Turner in 1831, was fueled by Christian rhetoric of freedom and divine justice. Laws were passed in the South, making it illegal to teach Blacks to read. Almost everywhere slaves met was monitored by owners, however, slaves continued to conduct their own meetings hidden or disguised in what was called "invisible institutions." By 1861, when the battle of Bull Run was fought, membership surged to 200,000 black members in the Methodist Episcopal Church and 150,000 Black Baptist. After the Civil War, and aided by the Freedman's Aid Society in 1880, nearly one million Black Baptist were worshipping in their own churches (Mead 1840).

Today the Black Baptist Preacher is an American icon with his or her own distinct style! This Southern Baptist style is lively, entertaining, forceful, and presents the Word of God in clear and easy to understand sermons.

This and all Baptist denominations keep our *Stew* fresh and inviting. It, perhaps more so then any other group, reflects the atmosphere and taste of American denominationalism. Hot, spicy, and full of life!

CATHOLIC CHURCH

Rich in history and tradition, the Catholic Churches view themselves as the unbroken continuity of the Christian faith from the Apostle Peter up to the present. Whether they are a denomination of Christianity or an entire religion within themselves is cause for debate. Either way, "they are the largest [by numbers] religious organization in America" (Mead 77) and by far, the world's largest Catholic organization is the Roman Catholic Church (the R.R.C.).

According to most, the history of the Catholic Church for the last two-thousand years is basically the history of Western Christianity. Ever since its official conception during the 4th century (by Constantine of Rome, see Catholic Church in INDEX for more) the writings of its Church Fathers have instructed in scripture, in Christian life, Catholic doctrine, ritual, practice and tradition. "It was during the Patristic Age [the period between the deaths of the Apostles to the close of the 8th century] that most of the Catholic doctrine and policy was established" (Mead).

During this period, there were no divisions between Eastern and Western Catholicism. The divisions developed later, due in part, to liturgical and administrative practices. The Eastern culture (the Byzantines) tended to define the Church in terms of fundamental orthodox practices, while the West (the Roman Church) focused on institutional allegiances during the social chaos of the middle ages.

Because the Church of the West was the only body strong enough to provide protection and direction during the barbarian onslaught of the Goths, Vandals, Franks and Saxons of the 5th century, it gained authority and power, emerging as the central power structure of the time. Because it (the Church of the West) became the unifying force amid chaos the word "Catholic," which is Latin for *"Universal,"* was increasingly applied to those loyal to the Bishop of Rome (Mead 78).

By 1204, and after the 4th Crusade, the break between East and West was complete. The Church in the East continued to decline, especially after the final conquest of Constantinople by the Turks. The Church in the West moved back to Rome and became the Roman Catholic Church---while the Eastern Church became known as the Greek Orthodox Church.

In all of Western history, the Roman Catholic Church was the most significant force in shaping Christianity as we know it---especially in the wake of Luther's Protestant Reformation. Without the R.C.C. there would never have been Protestantism: nothing to protest against! Even with the strength of the Protestants and a somewhat shady political history, the R.C.C. has retained its core doctrines and traditions in America.

Not all Roman Catholics believe the same things. Ultratraditonal Catholics defend old-time Catholicism and are critical of changes brought about by the Vatican: Traditionalist Catholics generally accept the reforms of the Vatican, while Liberal Catholics tend to replace the Bible and Church authority with the authority of human reason and question the Pope, Church Councils, and in some instances even the Bible itself. Charismatic and Evangelical Catholics affirm most conservative doctrines while emphasizing the gifts of the Holy Spirit, the importance of being Baptized in the Spirit and the Spirit-Filled Life: Cultural Catholics (also called "womb to the tomb" Catholics) are born, baptized, married and buried in the traditions of the Church. Although they are relatively unconcerned about spirituality, all social aspects of their culture and life center on Catholic tradition and expected behavior (Rhodes 99-100).

Even with all the diversity among Catholics they have still retained many of the same traditions and doctrinal beliefs. There are volumes of these and the following is just a small sample of Catholic practices and beliefs:

Beliefs & Practices

---Salvation is through Jesus Christ but one must be a member of the Catholic Church to enter into Heaven:

---Infallibility of the Pope. The R.C.C. enlist a strict hierarch (The Pope, to Priest and so on). The belief is that the office of the Pope, the highest office in the Catholic Church, is an unbroken chain of Divine Authority from the Apostle Peter to the present? The Pope is God's sole representative on this earth:

---Celibacy of the Priesthood. The priest must remain unmarried and abstain from all sexual behavior. There is currently debate on this issue, which may result in a major rift in the institution itself. The principal is that, like Catholic Nuns, the Catholic Priest must remain unmarried because they are symbolically married to the Church. Anything that would distract them from total devotion to the Church is disallowed:

---Veneration of Mary. The virgin Mary, mother of Jesus, is regarded as having been immaculately conceived herself, thus born without sin. She remained perpetually a virgin even after giving birth to Jesus in Bethlehem. Mary is referred to as "Mother of God" and seen as co-redeemer and co-mediator of grace. At the end of her life she was "assumed" into heaven where she stands today with Jesus answering prayers and administrating grace and miracles:

---The Bible is the written Word of God, including

seven "Apocryphal" books contained in the Catholic Bible:

---Baptism is required for membership into the Church and membership is required for admittance into Heaven. It is usually administered to infants by pouring or sprinkling while anointing them with Holy Oil on the forehead:

---Confirmation is required of all practicing members and after completing the required catechism the Confirmation is completed by the laying on of hand of a priest:

---Confession and Penitence. After hearing one's confession of sins the Priest can assign "penitence;" a special saying or deeds designed to show repentance for sin(s):

---Holy Communion (the "Eucharist") is the central act of Catholic devotion. This giving of wine and bread differs from Protestant Communion or the Lord's Supper in that the Catholic principal is that the wine actually turns into Christ' blood and the bread (the Eucharist) turns into Jesus' flesh. This is called "transubstantiation:"

---Marriage and Divorce. Since marriage is a holy sacrament it cannot be dissolved by any human power, thus, divorce is not allowed.

Along with the multitude of traditions, doctrines, and various Catholic beliefs not mentioned here, *The Official Catholic Directory 2000* list a total of 137 religious orders for men and 441 for women. These "Orders" differ in their work, from contemplative monasteries, cloistered convents, schools, mission work, administrative and curators of religious artifacts. For example, the "Order of Conhoniana" in West Africa; the "Order of San Francis Agis" in Mexico; the "Order of Maria Clara" (for women) in the Philippines; the "Jesuits," the "Dominicans," and so on to name just a few.

Ever since the first Catholic missionaries came to the Americas with the Spanish and French explorers (the first permanent Catholic Parish was in St. Augustine, Florida in 1565), Catholic Orders and traditions have helped mold Christianity in the United States. Everything from the stained glass Cathedrals in our major cities down to the dusty stucco missions on Indian reservations---from the pomp and grandeur of the Pope to the humbleness of the orphanage nuns---Catholicism is as much a part of America as hot dogs at a baseball game.

Whether one agrees with Catholic practices or not, it does not negate the fact that Catholicism was here first. While Protestantism was the wind that brought the early settlers to this New Land, Catholic Priest and explorers reached Her before them. The Catholic ritual, their grandeur, their history and their influence can be tasted in every spoonful of this *Great American Denominational Stew* of Christianity we love so much.

CHRISTIAN SCIENTIST

A purely American created Church, the official title is "the Church of Christ, Scientist," is also one of the few denominations founded by a woman. A woman named Mary Baker Eddy (1821-1910). The main thrust of this odd denomination is Faith Healing: healing without medication, drugs, surgery, or any physician direction. "Generally described as a religious teaching and practice based on the words and work of Christ Jesus, its founder [Mary Eddy] regarded it as the scientific system of divine healing and rule of universal harmony" (Mead 356). Move over Edger Casey!

After surviving a lifetime of illnesses and failed marriages, Mary Eddy had taken a fall on a slippery sidewalk in 1866 and was pronounced "incurable" and given three days to live by the attending physician, Doctor Alvin M. Cushing. On the third day, allegedly her last, Mary cried out for a Bible. After reading Matthew 9:2 where Jesus heals a man ill with palsy, Mary rose completely healed! "It was at that moment, it's claimed, that she discovered Christian Science" (Martin 133). It quickly grew to include its own publishing company, College of Healing, and a tightly controlled network of Churches. (See INDEX for more on Eddy).

Although Christian Science does not accept that Jesus died on the cross, rose on the third day, and was the sacrificial lamb given for atonement for our sins, they still call themselves "Christian" because they use the Christian *Bible* as a source book and use the healings of Christ and the Disciples as models.

They use the *Bible* but do not accept it as inerrant. They do not believe in the Trinity but in one God---the "I Am"---Jesus and the Holy Ghost are forces of the "I Am... Illnesses are not healed by declaring it so, but rather by knowing that there is no sickness, only mistakes in understanding (kind of a Gnostic thing). Likewise, evil is only false belief: believing anything other than truth is evil and leads to illness and a failed life. Prayer cannot change God's design so basically it's objectionable. They deny the existence of Satan, since evil is only the result of false beliefs and/or thinking. If we falsely believe in Satan, it is an evil act and we reap the negative results of it just as if there were actually an evil Satan tormenting us.

Basically, Christian Science is attractive to many "trendy" people who are dissatisfied with the traditional doctrine of God's total sovereignty and our sinful nature. The Church of Christian Science has grown rapidly in these last-of-days. Its worldwide ministry has become a household word in America. Because of its denial of Jesus as Savior and its rejection of the power of the Holy Ghost, it easily falls into a chief position as a cult. The Apostle John would take it a step further and call it "not Christian" but "antichrist" because they deny Jesus as Savior:

> *"For many deceivers are entered into the world who confess not that Jesus Christ is come in the flesh. This is a deceiver and an antichrist."* (II John 7) see also (1 John 2:22)

Agree with it or not, it carries the title "Christian" in its name and the world has added it to our *Great Denominational Stew.* So like many other suspicious things in our *Stew,* like a worm infested potato or a chunk of poison mushroom, we need to partake carefully…careful to not eat it up or take it inside of us. We could end up deathly ill…or is that a false belief too?

<u>CHURCH OF CHRIST</u>

The Church of Christ does not consider itself a denomination. They, like many other groups we will look at, "claim to be the original Church" prepared by Jesus Himself. J. Harvey Dykes, author of *"The Church of Christ Established,"* puts it this way; "The history of Jesus' Church is not the history of a denomination. Jesus' church was not a denomination…it began before any denomination was bore" (p. 13).

"They prefer to call it the 'Restored Movement' or the 'return to New Testament' Christianity" (Baxter 3). They do not have a Reformist of Separatist history filled with spiritual minded truth-seekers who saw that the Church described in the New Testament had drifted far off course. "These men did not advocate the starting of a new church but rather a return to Christ' Church as described in the Bible" (Baxter 4). This would make them "Purist" in an exact sense of the word.

One of the earliest advocates of this Restoration Movement was the American, James O'Kelly, of the Methodist Episcopal Church. In 1793, he withdrew from his Church in Baltimore and called on others to join him in taking the Bible as "the only creed." In 1802 Thomas Campbell and his son, Alexander, contended, "Nothing should be thrust upon Christians as a matter of doctrine if it's not as old as the New Testament" (Baxter 4). When the Second Great Awakening swept through Tennessee and Kentucky, preaching focused on the need for conversion rather than on denominational distractions. The motto was, "Deeds over Creeds."

Another motto, this one credited to Thomas Campbell when he and his son founded a group called "The Christian Association of Washington County," was "Where the scriptures speak, we speak: where the scriptures are silent, we are silent" (Rhodes 114). In a sense, these early leaders, the Campbells, the Jones, Smith, and O'Kelly, were a new breed of Separatist…not separating from the R.C.C. but separation from all denominations. Seeing a need to separate true believers from denominationalist, they came up with six basic Christian ideals:

1) Christ is the only head of the Church.

2) The Bible is sufficient rule for faith and practice.

3) Christian character is the measure of membership.

4) A correct individual interpretation of scripture is a way of life.

5) "Christian" is the name taken for followers of Christ.

6) Unity: Christians working together for the common good. (Mead 250).

By 1832, an argument over statement number five (above) split the believers into two groups: "Stoneites" and "Campbellites." The Stoneites favored the name "Christians" while the Campbellites like "Disciples" better. Over time, two distinct fellowships emerged under the title "Christian Churches:" the Christian Church (Disciples of Christ) and the Christian Church (Church of Christ). Both still rejected the designation as a denomination.

By 1906, the disunity had forced another split. The final straw was the issue of instrumental music (including organs) in Church. The conservatives who opposed instrumental music because it is not found within the pages of the New Testament stuck with the name "Church of Christ," while the progressives who allowed music adopted the name "Disciples of Christ."

Both groups hold to baptism by immersion, clinging to the teaching that baptism is only for adults who profess "Jesus is Lord." Baptism brings remission of sins (mandatory for forgiveness) and is a condition for church membership. The Eucharist is served every Sunday as a memorial and a sacred act of obedience. The Church does not believe in original sin but does recognize that all people are sinful (Rhodes 117-120).

Due to their great devotion to Christ, they have become a stable part of our *Great Denominational Stew*...even if they deny being in it.

EPISCOPAL (Anglican)

The Protestant Reformation historically began in 1517 when Martin Luther nailed his *95 Thesis* to the door of the castle in Wittenberg. Thirteen years later, in 1530, King Henry VIII of England wanted to divorce his wife (Catherine of Aragon) but the Pope said "No!' Fueled by the Reformation, King Henry not only kicked the Roman Catholic Church out of England but also claimed all the Churches for the State. He renamed them "the Churches of England," with the King as their head rather than a Pope.

Although Henry VIII was first to reject Papal supremacy, his successors, Edward VI and Elizabeth, I made the Church of England clearly Protestant (Mead 102). Out of this, by 1611, England had its own *Bible* in English (the KJV) and the Church (Called the "Anglican" or "Episcopal") eventually had its *"Book of Common Prayer* and the *"Thirty-Nine Articles of Faith"* to guide it. "The Church of England was firmly established and quickly became an influential religious body in the world" (Rhodes 139).

The Episcopal Church is so named because it is governed by Bishops. The Greek word *"episkipso"* means "bishops" or "overseers." It is also called Anglican because *"Anglican"* literally means "English" (Rhodes 140). The Episcopal Church finally emerged on American soil as an extension of the Church of England. (See INDEX for more on Anglicans).

The first Anglican Church was founded by English (therefore the name "Anglican") in 1617 in Jamestown, Virginia. The name "Church of England" was avoided while "Episcopal" or "Anglican" was encouraged. As settlers came into the new World, the Anglican Churches continued to crop up on the landscape: Boston in 1689, Philadelphia in 1695, New York City in 1697, and Newport RI in 1702. By the end of the colonial period, Anglican Churches were in all 13 colonies and by 1775; there were some 400 Anglican congregations on American soil (Rhodes 140).

This caused a major crisis related to the American War for Independence. One simply cannot fight England while at the same time maintaining allegiance to the Crown through the Episcopal system of its Churches. This predicament caused a major split among Anglican clergy in America. "Many would rather close their parishes than remove prayer for the King from the Churches liturgy" (Rhodes 140).

In true American fashion, a remnant survived and decided to regroup and establish a denomination independent of the Church of England, just as the colonies were seeking to be independent of the government of England. They wanted to form a Church, which would be completely autonomous (Rhodes 141). The bigger problem was that they had no way to ordain and consecrate new priest without the Bishops in England and there was still that annoying "praying for the King" rule.

By 1789 the problem was solved. The home Church in England finally rescinded the requirement that "all Bishops must pray for and swear allegiance to the British Crown." Two American priest (soon to become Bishops) William White and Samuel Provest, sailed to England and were consecrated by the Archbishop of Canterbury.

That same year the American Church adopted a constitution, ratified canons, and was allowed to revise the *Book of Common Prayer* for use in American Anglican Churches. This is considered the formal beginnings of the Episcopal Church in the United States of America (Rhodes 142).

NOTE: it was first called the "Protestant Episcopal Church" but later drifted back to its more common name, the "Episcopal Church in America."

As for today's Churches, the Episcopalian Church has thrived on American soil. Under its heritage several sub-denominations have emerged: Communion of Charismatic Episcopal Churches: and its oldest and still largest, the Episcopal Church in America. Each has its own personality and local beliefs, customs, and traditions, but they all closely adhere to the basic Episcopalian doctrine:

Beliefs & Practices

---They use *The Apostle's Creed*: *The Nicene Creed*: *The Thirty-Nine Articles of Faith*: (amended to avoid swearing loyalty to England): *The Book of Common Prayer*: as well as *The Bible*:

---The *Bible*, Old and New Testaments, are God's written Word, therefore they must be interpreted apart from tradition and reason:

---God is the Creator and head of the Trinity:

---Original sin corrupted man and continues to do so:

---Through the life, death, and resurrection of Jesus our sins can be forgiven:

---The Sacraments of Baptism and the Eucharist are ordained by Christ:

---Baptism can be performed by pouring, sprinkling, or by immersion:

---The righteous will have eternal life with God while the unrighteous will experience eternal death and separation from God.

Recently the Episcopal Church in America has been rocked by political unrest, resulting in major internal splits. "In 2003 the denomination concreted its first woman Bishop, Katharine Schori" and then its first openly gay Bishop, V. Gean Robinson of New Hampshire" (Fort Worth Star, Nov. 5, 2006, p. 16A). This break with the traditional interpretation of Scripture and the *Book of Common Prayer,* according to Special Consultant Tim Jones of the Star Telegram (July 26, 2006, p. 7B) has already caused many dioceses to withdraw from under the banner of the main body. "This includes dioceses in Texas, Arkansas, Oklahoma, New Mexico, Kansas, and some in Missouri and Louisiana." The Episcopalian, as we know it, may evolve into something very different right before our eyes! Like Cain, Babel, and even Martin Luther, they are changing things around. We are witnessing history in the making.

As for our *Stew*, this denomination is like an old hand-me-down recipe our ancestors brought over from the Mother Land. Episcopalian/Anglican Churches bring an old-time flavor; a foreign characteristic to our Great *Denominational Stew*. A kind of forbidden taste---but still one of Christian substance and a vital part of Christian history that makes our *Stew* "American" rather than an import.

FRIENDS (Quakers)

Dating back to the 1650's in England, The Society of Friends (Quakes) is an unconventional but esteemed Protestant body (Mead 159). Their beginning is rooted in one man who lived in the

17th century England: the mystic preacher, George Fox (Latourette 822-23).

After suffering years of spiritual conflict while seeking authentic Christian faith, Fox (1625-1691), experienced the revelation of what he termed "the inner light." Fox came to believe that God gives every person a gift of divine inner light and depending on how they respond, they can receive more guidance through revelation (Rhodes 157). As Fox gathered followers, they were ridiculed and met with fierce opposition. When Fox was hauled into court he boldly advised the Judge to "tremble and quake at the word of the Lord!" The name "Quaker," meant in jest by those present, stuck (Mead 160). (For more on Fox see INDEX).

In spite of ridicule and persecution, Fox kept preaching the right of freedom of speech, the right to worship, and the right to refuse to take oaths or go to war. "From 1650 to 1689 more than three thousand suffered for the movement and three to four hundred died in prisons. When Fox died in 1691 the Quakers numbered fifty thousand" (Mead 160).

The Society of Friends soon brought the movement to the American colonies. As had happened earlier in England, it didn't find a hearty welcome at first. Some were accused of being Witches; others were whipped and ran out of town…four were even hanged in Boston. In 1667 William Penn became a convert to the Quakers and in 1681 was given land in America, which became known as Pennsylvania. After the passage of the "Act of Tolerance" in 1689, Pennsylvania became the safe haven and prime destination for Quakers coming to the New Land.

Penn used the colonies in Pennsylvania as his "Holy Experiment," allowing religious freedom to all who settled there. "This was a mile-stone on the path to full religious freedom in the American constitution" (Mead 160). The Quakers settled down to the business of farming and became well organized. It was a time of creativity, of growth, of mystical knowledge, and they quickly developed a strong identity in American government.

In these early years the Friends were basically a closed community, not totally cut off from the outside like the Amish aspire to be, but they held to strict rules of Godly living and failed members were shunned or disowned completely.

Influenced by the revival movement of the 19th century, most Friends abandoned the "quietism" of Quaker life and entered other areas of Christian endeavors such as evangelism and temperance, service to God, and the abolition of slavery. "They had purged their own society of slavery years in advance of any other religious body in the USA and the writings of Friends John Woolman (1710-70) and John C. Whittier (1807-92) helped to further the abolition movement in American society" (Mead 161).

As time passed, a number of Friends-affiliations emerged; the Evangelical Friends International, the Friends General Conference, the Friends United Meetings, and the Religious Society of Friends (conservative). During World War I friends from these affiliations and various churches pulled together to work in the "American Friends Service Committee" (A.F.S.C.) in relief and reconstruction efforts aboard. The A.F.S.C. remains today one of the most effective of such agencies in the world and in 1947 was jointly awarded the Nobel Peace Prize with its British counterpart.

Beliefs & Practices

As for beliefs and practices, the Friends are diverse but, like many other denominations, hold common beliefs:

> ---The Inner Light is the heart of Quaker theology and practice:

> ---They seek Holiness, but not perfection, which is a higher and more spiritual standard:

---Truth is an unfolding and continuing process which leads one to value the *Bible* but prefer to rely on the individual guidance of the Spirit of God, which is the same spirit which produced the *Bible* in the first place:

---Church worship is "un-programmed." Friends worship in silence until one is lead by the Spirit to speak:

---No pastors are needed as no outward sacraments (generally) are observed, although for orderly operations a pastor is assigned:

---Generally, Conservative Quakers do allow women to speak and even take on the role of pastors when the need arises:

---Salvation is received by grace through faith in Jesus and is evidenced by obedience and good works:

---Those that fall away can lose their salvation and fellowship with the Society.

While favoring extremely modest clothing, sporting beards and a quite demeanor, these Friends are raging spiritual warriors who confront evil head on with the faith of David and his sling! It is this fierce sense of purpose and spiritual guidance that characterizes the Quakers in our American History. Their unique flavor of spirituality adds an enduring quality to our *Great American Denominational Stew*; a mystical taste that joins history with contemporary America.

JEHOVAH'S WITNESSES

"The Jehovah's Witnesses are among the most zealous religious bodies in terms of promotion of their beliefs" (Mead 267). The most obvious element of this group is their insistence on using the name "Jehovah" rather than "God," relying on Isaiah 43:12 as their guide.

The modern history of Jehovah's Witnesses began more than one-hundred years ago with an inconspicuous Bible Study in Alleghency, Pennsylvania. By 1870 they had transformed the group into a "society" and published the first issue of *"Zion's Watchtower Magazine."* Two years later, the Zion's Watchtower Tract Society" was formed. It was incorporated in 1884 with Charles Taze Russell as their first president.

"Russell was deeply influenced by Adventist thought which had captured American attention around the mid 1800's. He developed his own Adventist ideas based on personal studies of the *Bible"* (Mead 268). By 1939 the name of the corporation was officially changed to "The Watchtower Bible & Tract Society" and remains one of the world's largest publishers of religious material.

The vast amount of literature the Witnesses produce (all without by-lines or any personal recognition) quotes extensively from their own translation called *"The New World Translation,"* revised and completed in 1961 (Martin 71). By modern times the Watchtower Society had emerged into a world-recognized denomination with its very own Bible, its own beliefs, its own doctrine, and its own station in the halls of American Christianity.

Beliefs & Practices

Some of the major doctrine and which separate them from other denominations are:

> ---They do not use the word "Church" but identify their place of worship as "Kingdom Hall:"

> ---They do not believe the Holy Spirit is a person possessing intellect, emotion, or will (Berry 35):

> ---Rather than the word "God" or "Yahweh," they

insist on using "Jehovah" when referring to the Creator:

---Jesus is not God but is a divine spirit-creature, like an angel, who put on the tent of flesh and dwelt among men:

---"Hell" is not a fiery place of torment, but is the common grave for all mankind until the resurrection:

---After judgment the lost do not suffer eternal punishment but simply cease to exist, which is eternal separation from Jehovah:

---Jesus returned from Heaven in 1914 and proceeded to overthrow Satan's organization:

---The Kingdom of God is superior to any earthly government---all of which are under Satan's Kingdom---so to swear allegiance to any government is to swear allegiance to Satan (Martin 51):

---The dead are conscious of absolutely nothing so their only hope is the resurrection of the dead... and the 144,000 of Revelation 7 is the number of Witnesses who will rule with Jesus...other Witnesses will populate God's new Kingdom:

In 1977 one of the last organizational changes made by the president at the time, N.N. Knorr before he died, was to enlarge the governing body and fully establish the headquarters in Brookland, N.Y. Since then their many schools, missionary boards, conventions, successful court cases, volumes of literature, their refusal to salute the flag, to bear arms in war, or to participate in political office have made their society a household name.

Like them or not---agree or disagree with their beliefs---their sincerity and passivism brings a certain mellowing flavor with it.

Like a backyard garden, the Witnesses, are a homegrown American denomination who have become a huge ingredient in our *Great American Stew* of Christianity.

LUTHERAN

"Lutheran Churches emerged from the teachings and writings of Martin Luther (1484-1546) who is sometimes called the "Father of Protestantism" (Rhodes 24). Luther, an Augustinian Monk and teacher, began uncovering significant differences between the teachings of the Bible and those of the Roman Catholic Church. In 1517 he posted his famous *"95 Thesis"* to the door of Wittenberg Castle's Church hoping to bring reform to the Church, but ended up bringing division instead.

Luther was excommunicated by the Pope himself. His followers used the term "Lutheran" as a badge of honor---but his enemies used it as synonymous with traitor. He wrote (often in codified form) of what he called *"The Large Catechism"* and *"The Small Catechism."* From 1537 and on he was devoted almost exclusively to writing tracts, books and hymns, including his masterpiece, *"A Mighty Fortress Is Our God"*. He even translated the *Latin Bible* into English and had it printed on the new Gutenberg printing press. His reformist ideas struck a match in the hearts of men that spread over Europe like wildfire.

After his, death in 1546, his followers debated some finer points of his theology and quickly consolidated Lutheran Orthodoxy, that is, "theology according to Luther's works," into a single book titled *"The Book of Concord."* ("Concord" means "agreement" or "unity of mind"). This core book contained the *Apostle's Creed*, the *Augsburg Confession*, Luther's *Small & Large Catechisms*, and the *Smalcald Articles of Faith* (Rhodes 213-14).

This book, the *Book of Concord*, became the unifying point of many Protestants and they in turn formed groups known as "Lutherans." These groups grew into churches by the same name.

Even today, most Lutheran Churches still hold this book in high esteem, but others have departed and grown toward a more liberal theology.

The first Lutherans to migrate to America in colonial days came from Germany, Sweden and Holland. "Their first Lutheran Christmas service was held at Hudson Bay in 1619" (Mead 113). They settled and spread out as the nation grew, mostly gathering in Pennsylvania, New York, North Carolina, Maryland, Delaware and on into Ohio. These early Lutherans were openly Protestant and it showed in the structure of their newly found Churches.

Rather than a Pope or governing council who issues directives, the local church was, and still is, the basic Lutheran government. "Churches own their own property and select their own Pastors" (Rhodes 214). Each Church elects members to a "synod" (meaning, "walking together") which serves as a local group of church representatives who "walk together" in governing the Church much like Elders, Deacons, or Board Members of other denominations. Sometimes these Synods gather in large bodies called "Conferences" and produce great works for the common good of the Churches.

For example, one Conference founded the "Lutheran World Relief" through which more than $300 million in cash and food has been distributed throughout the world (Mead 114). Through their Synod and conference system uniting various bodies, they are active in education, publication, charity, missions, and even legislative influence on national as well as state and local levels (Mead 115).

Beliefs & Practices

In spite of some division there has been solid unity among most Lutherans based more on faith than on denominational concerns. They believe, though faith, that:

---The *Bible* is the inerrant Word of God:

---Jesus is the redeemer, He died on the cross, rose, ascended to Heaven and sits at the right hand of God:

---After Adam and Eve's fall from innocence, all humans are born into the world with a sin nature:

---The "Law" is used to make us aware of sin and sin can be overcome through faith in Jesus:

---A new life can be obtained after baptism and baptism can be by sprinkling, pouring or by immersion:

---Christ is present during the Lord's Supper but the elements do not themselves change, God only uses them to communicate grace to the receiver:

---An outstanding feature is that they believe "Repentance leads to faith," whereas the Reformed position today is that "Repentance flows from faith" (Walton 71).

There were at one time 150 different Lutheran bodies in the USA, through consolidation, unification, and federation during the 20th century the number was reduced to fewer than a dozen. For example, in 1968 the "American Lutheran Church" merged with the "Lutheran Church in America" to form the "Evangelical Lutheran Church in America." And as usually happens with denominational mergers, new separate ones are also formed in protest. In spite of some divisions, the Lutheran Church remains a solid ingredient in *America's Denominational Stew*. It gives it stability and that good old-fashioned fragrance that makes it American *Stew*.

MENNONITE & AMISH

The Mennonite Church was established during the early Protestant Reformation. Reformers such as Martin Luther in Germany, Zwingli in Switzerland, Knox in Scotland, Calvin in France and many others had risen up to denounce the Catholic Church and cry out for a return to the *Bible* (Rod 2). Movements formed by people who followed these great leaders...these great men of faith.

By the 1520's a group, which rejected the idea of "reforming" the Catholic Church or the established Church of England, emerged. Rather than reform---rather than fixing something they saw as broken beyond repair---they wanted total separation. Separation from churches of the day and get back to the basics of worship earned them the label of "Separatist."

One group, which had formed under the banner of Ulrich Zwingli in Zurich, Switzerland, pulled away when he tried to compromise on the issue of infant baptism (Funk & Wagnall vol. 17, p 177). Their position was that infant baptism is unscriptural, that baptism can only be performed upon (or after) conversion and one must be old enough to make a conscious decision to do so. Because of this--- the practice of "re-baptizing" believers who had been baptized as infants---they were called "Anabaptist" or "Rebaptizers."

Frank S. Mead, author of the text, "Handbook of Denominations" (12th ed.), tells, "The first Anabaptist congregation of historical record were those out of Zurich who in 1525 had rejected the teachings of Zwingli" (148). On January 21, 1525, on the basis of confession of faith," the brethren of believers baptized one another and were called "Anabaptist" (Rod 5). Later in 1536, a priest from Holland named Menno Simons, renounced Catholicism and joined the Protestant movement of the Anabaptist.

Through his strong leadership ability many Anabaptist united under him. Through skillful writings and bold faith, Menno Simons defended their faith against the skewed traditions of Catholicism of the day---against Protestants who were willing to compromise— against anyone who challenged the faith of the brethren. These brethren identified with his name and became known as "Menno-nites." The main concern of the Mennonites was not so much with theology, sacraments or the liturgy, but that they believed themselves called to exemplify godly living based on the *Sermon On The Mount* and taught Matthew 5 6 &7 fervently.

The prime example of ultra-conservative Christianity, the Mennonites dedicated their lives in piety and humbleness while segregating themselves into communities securely blocked from the wicked influences of the outside world. After suffering harassment and persecutions, many fled to America in search of religious freedom.

Sympathetic to their cause a Quaker named William Penn offered them a safe haven in the new territory named after himself: "Pennsylvania." The humble Mennonites gladly accepted and were among the first to settle Germantown, Pennsylvania. By 1683 thousands had immigrated to America and not only to Pennsylvania's Lancaster County, but on into Ohio, Virginia, the West and up into Canada (Rhodes 239 & Mead 149).

Today Mennonites (out of which the Amish later emerged) have split several times, resulting in different branches: Old Order, General Conference, Mennonite Brethren, Beachy Amish Mennonites, Wislers, and a few others.

Beliefs & Practices

Some of their beliefs may vary slightly from group to group, but some general beliefs are:

---No lawsuits against Christians (I Cor. 6:1-8):

---No outside marriages (II Cor. 6:14):

---No conformity with the world (John 15:19 & 1 John 2:15-16):

---No worldly entertainment (Heb 11:25 & Rom 8:13):

---No wearing of gold or immodest apparel (1 Tim 2:9-10):

---Women should have long hair (1 Cor 11:6):

---Use of anointing oil for the sick (Mark 10:11-12):

---Obedience to the *"Dordrecht Confession of Faith,"* composed in 1632 in the Netherlands.

At first glance, Old style Quakers, Old Order Mennonites, and typical **Amish** all have the same general appearance, but the Amish are distinguished by more than their clothes. Their extremely segregated lifestyle sets them apart from all others today. The Amish church separated itself from industrial and materialistic society and even though they originated from the Mennonites, they separated from even them as being "too worldly."

"Emerging in the 1720's out of the teaching of the 17th century Swiss Mennonite, Bishop Jakab Amman" (Rhodes 260) they couldn't come into full agreement so they split into two main groups; "Old Order Amish" and "New Order Amish." The New Order was open to a more progressive lifestyle and accepting social change while the Old Order (the more conservative group) held onto the old ways (Rhodes 260). Different yet alike, both branches share common beliefs:

---They dress in severely plain style clothing using hooks and eyes instead of buttons:

---They ride in horse-drawn buggies and avoid (when possible) machinery of any type, including automobiles:

---They don't have a telephone line into their communities because the line would "connect" them with the outside world:

---The males are bearded and females wear long hair and a head covering:

---Religious services are held in homes where a communion service is held regularly:

---Marriage to an outsider is strictly prohibited:

---Discipline is enforced by shunning (Funk & Wagnall Vol. 12, p 89).

Persecuted in Europe, the Amish migrated in the 18th century to Pennsylvania where their descendents are called "Pennsylvania Dutch." They are spread out mainly in the Midwestern United States and up into Canada. Where they go they maintain their rural agriculture lifestyle and segregation.

The Amish and Mennonites bring a healthy flavor to our Stew. Their purity brings a wholesomeness that fills the heart as it conjures up memories of clean living and days gone by. Without them our *Great American Stew* would be just another copy---but with them in the mix it is unique---a taste of bold freedom in the spirit of piety in action.

METHODIST

"With the possible exception of the Reformed Churches, the Methodist have been the most influential Protestant family of Churches in the United States. Hundreds of American Denominations, service organizations, and educational institutions have their roots in the Methodist movement" (Mead 27).

Beginning as a pietist movement within the Church of England in the 1730's, Methodism expanded during the 18th century under the leadership of the Wesley brothers, John (1703-91) and Charles (1707-88) who preached and wrote hymns on the need for personal salvation and change in life. John Wesley, the first child of an Anglican Rector in Epworth, Lincolnshire, was trained at Oxford University. Around 1729 he and his younger brother, Charles, began methodically meeting with a group at a stated time for ordered prayer and study. Because they were so methodical---meeting precisely on time and following a systematical regimen of prayer and reading---they soon acquired the name of Methodist (Rhodes 263).

John was ordained a deacon in the Church of England in1728 and after his father passed away, he returned to Oxford and was ordained a priest in 1735. Later that year he and Charles visited America as Missionaries. While on a ship they met some Moravian Christians whose simple piety and morality greatly impressed them. After returning to England, John kept in touch with them and in 1738 attended a Moravian service in London.

There he experienced a religious awakening that would change his life. "His religion was no longer just an intellectual faith but rather a personal relationship with God Himself" (Rhodes 264). He gained a new direction---the revitalization of church life in England. His somewhat unorthodox approach to this was not welcome in the Anglican pulpits. So after encouragement from evangelist George Whitefield, he began preaching "in open air."

He preached in open fields, on street corners, and at town squares. He preached to the poor, to the downtrodden, and to anyone who would listen. His message was much like Whitfield's: repent, regeneration, and justification by faith. His converts form "Societies," usually in private homes, where members supported each other and were accountable to one another rather than to a Church Board. In 1739, John Wesley drew up a set of General Rules that are still held by modern Methodist as an ideal of Biblical rules of conduct.

By the mid 1760's Methodism had been established in the United States. In 1769 Methodist in New York had built the Wesley Chapel, now known as John Street Methodist Church. This period of

Methodist growth in America produced many names, many whose works are still used today in seminaries. Names such as Charles Webb (1772-96), Devarevy Jarrett (1733-1801), Francis Ashbury (1795-1826), and Thomas Roakin (1738-1810). When the Methodist Church broke free of both England and the Church of England to become an American Church in its own right, ordained Ministers appointed Asbury and Thomas Coke as superintendents (Mead 219).

This brought Methodism into the age of circuit riders: preachers on horseback. The *Methodist Book of Concord"* was established in 1789 and put in the saddlebags of these riders. The revivalist flavor of the camp meeting (John Wesley's open-air style) became popular with Methodist and by the mid 1800's there were 1.3 million Methodist in America. (Mead 219). Since then they have grown and split into various groups several times, especially over the issue of slavery, but in 1939 the vast majority of Methodist and Methodist Episcopal Churches united in Kansas City and formed the official "Methodist Church" as we know it today.

They settled on three major doctoral statements, which defined Methodist belief and practice:

1) The *Apostle's Creed*---which is often recited during services. (See this in "CREEDS").

2) The *25 Articles of Religion*---which is John Wesley's revision of the *39 Articles* of the Church of England (see page 41 for more on this).

3) The *Doctrines & Discipline of the Methodist Church*---which is re-issued every four years.

Belief & Practices

Some of the other beliefs and practices of the Methodist Church are:

---They reject the Calvinist emphases on predestination

and lean more toward Arminianism, which emphasizes free will and salvation, open to all:

---Although they subscribe to Wesley's doctrine of perfection, (the idea that one can be enabled by the Holy Spirit to say "no" to sin and become perfect in love), they preach the doctrine of man's sinful nature:

---They follow the Trinity teaching of God in three persons:

---Follow the doctrine of justification by faith alone:

---The sufficiency of scriptures for identifying salvation (no outside sources needed):

---Baptism can be administrated to both infants and adults, usually by sprinkling:

---Membership is based on confession of faith or by letter of transfer:

---Children must be 13 years of age for membership but this can be waved:

---Worship and liturgy are based on the *English Prayer Book*:

---Clergy are appointed by Bishops at the annual Conference, although each "Charge" elects its own administrative Board, planning, and policies at the local level.

Due to each Church being "in charge" of its own policies, Methodist (much like Baptist do) tend to have varying beliefs and practices. By tailoring to local, each Charge can pay close attention to quality of life rather than defending specific doctrine (Rhodes 266). This mode allows many different Methodist denominations to flourish. Groups such as the African Methodist Church with 1,857,000 adult members; the African Methodist Episcopal Zion Church with 1,430,000 members; the Christian Methodist Episcopal Church with 784,000 members; Congregational Methodist; Evangelical Methodist; Southern Methodist; and the largest one, the United Methodist Church which claims 8,251,000 members on its role.

NOTE: the Salvation Army was a Methodist Movement, which now has is its own Church and is an excellent example of John Wesley's interaction with focus on the poor and missionary functions. It is a genuine expression of modern day Moravian practices in action. (See Salvation Army in INDEX).

Another interesting branch of Methodism is the Wesleyan Methodist Church headquartered in Indianapolis, Indiana. It follows most standard Methodist tradition but in 1891 a "revival of holiness" swept the Methodist community resulting in many to focus on evangelism and missions. They formed the Wesleyan Methodist Convention of America, elected a missionary board and general missionary supervisors. In 1947, it had developed its own following and the name was changed to the "Wesleyan Methodist Church of America" and headquartered in Syracuse, New York. In 1957, it moved to Indiana where the Church has branched out internationally, still holding to its evangelism and missionary tradition (Office 6).

The Methodist Church with all its branches and groups stabilize our *Great American Stew*. They give it a hint of an imported texture while at the same time keeps that American flavor dominate in the soup. It not only feeds us but there is always enough left over for others as well. This has become an American trademark…feeding others with our *Stew*.

MORMONS

Popularly known as "Mormons," or "Latter Day Saints" (L.D.S.), members of the "Church of Jesus Christ of Latter Day Saints" are unique in Christianity. Their most outstanding feature is they base their beliefs not only on the Old and New Testaments of the *Bible*, but on three other books as well: *"The Book of Mormon, Doctrine & Covenants*, and *The Pearl of Great Price,"* all written by their founder, Joseph Smith Jr.

Although many place Mormons in the category of a cult (Martin 166) "few churches live with such clear identity and maintain such a high degree of loyalty and dedication" (Mead 346). Agree or disagree with their ways, it cannot take away the fact that Mormonism is an American creation and is growing bigger daily.

Unlike other denominations, Mormons are split into only two groups: 1. The "Church of Jesus Christ of Latter Day Saints" headquartered in Salt Lake City, Utah: and 2. The "Reorganized Church of Jesus Christ of Latter Day Saints" headquartered in Independence, Missouri. They are not so much split on doctrine as they are on historical tradition.

Although most Mormon doctrine differs radically from that of mainstream Christianity, they do call themselves "Christian" and use the name of "Jesus" in their denominational title. They do not consider Jesus as the Son of God but only as semi-divine. As Mormon scholar, Stephen Robinson puts it, "He [Jesus] has 46 chromosomes like everyone else---23 from God and 23 from the Virgin Mary" (Week 13). They consider America the Promised Land of scripture and are preparing themselves for Jesus' return to rule in the thousand years of peace. So how old is this semi-Christian faith?

It is less than 200 years old. The Mormon Church is rooted firmly in an 1820 vision of its founder, Joseph Smith Jr. It was in that year, while praying in the woods that he received a vision in which God the Father and Jesus materialized and spoke to him. The prophet (as he is called) recorded the incident in detail in his book, *"The Pearl of Great Price."* In it he revealed that the two "personages" took a dim view of the Christian Church and announced that a restoration of true Christianity was needed and that he, Joseph Smith, had been chosen to launch the new dispensation" (Martin 170).

In 1827, Smith claimed that an angel named "Moroni" had led him to a hill near Manchester, New York, where he was given (or dug up) a book written on golden plates which had been left there by an ancient prophet named "Mormon." Using a "seer stone" given him by the angel Moroni, Smith spent the next few years translating what he called the "reformed Egyptian hieroglyphics." "These plates contained the sacred records of ancient inhabitants of North America, righteous Jews who had fled from Jerusalem's Babylonian captivity in 600 BC and sailed to America in a divinely designed ark" (Mead 747).

In 1820, Smith published the 500 page *"Book of Mormon"* which is described as the last gospel of Jesus. From it Smith "concluded that Jackson County, Mo., was the site of both the Garden of Eden and the location of Jesus' second coming" (The Week 13).

This was Divine Providence at its extreme! It exploded in revival. People either loved it or hated it. Loved it because it placed America in the center of God's plan and promises---hated it because it, in practice, was contrary to traditional Biblical teachings. Smith's followers began practicing polygamy: Smith himself reportedly had as many as 40 wives. He was assaulted, jailed, and eventually killed by a lynch mob, leaving leadership to his successor, Brigham Young, to lead 30,000 Mormons out of harm's way and into Utah.

For decades the Mormons led a turbulent existence as separatist, lives marked with violent skirmishes with authorities, churches, other settlers, and even the government itself. Only in 1890, when they abolished polygamy did they, as Mormons, begin entering the American mainstream.

With 12 million members (8.5 in the USA) it is one of the fastest growing religions/denominations in the world. One explanation for the fast growth is that the birth rate in Utah is 50% higher than the national average. Mormons encourage large families, are family orientated, and live extremely healthy lifestyles compared to most contemporary Americans: no alcohol, no coffee, tea, and so on… The Mormon beliefs are not left at the Temple door on Sundays when services are over. Mormonism is a way of life---reaching every aspect of family life.

Beliefs & Practices

Some of the Mormon beliefs and practices are:

---All younger members are expected to devote two years to spreading the faith in foreign or domestic mission service:

---Three hour services every Sunday plus at least one evening weekly in educational meetings:

---No Divorce:

---The Trinity is the Father, Son and Holy Ghost, but the Father and Son have bodies of flesh and bones:

---Baptism is by immersion and is necessary for salvation:

---Baptism of the dead (by proxy) makes salvation possible for those, even non-Mormons, who died unsaved:

---The Holy Ghost can be received by the laying on of hands:

---The practice of the Lord's Supper is administered every Sunday:

---Like Pentecostals and other Charismatic's today, Mormons believe in the speaking of tongues, visions, prophecy, and healing by touch (Mead 748).

Rather one agrees with Mormon doctrine and theology or not, the Latter Day Saints are uniquely American. Its founder was born in

America, found the golden plates in America, published his books here, and had American followers. Brigham Young established the Church in Utah and America is seen as the Promised Land. You cannot get more American than that!

With all its rich and mystical history, Mormonism holds a keen place in the *Great American Stew* of Christian Denominationalism. It is a homegrown ingredient that adds that old familiar flavor of home cooking to our *Stew*.

NATIVE AMERICAN CHURCH

The Native American Church (NAC) began around the turn of the century with a man named "Quanah Parker." Parker was half-white and half-Indian. His mother, Cynthia, was white and raised in the Comanche way. When her Comanche husband died she was allowed to take her son, Quanah, and return to her people. Shortly after she returned to Texas, her son got deathly ill. The medical professionals couldn't help him so Cynthia, remembering the Indian Ways, took him to some Mexican-Indians.

They "cured" him by using peyote buttons. They also instructed Quanah in how to grow and use peyote for healing. He brought this knowledge back to the Comanche's in Texas.

Later he was converted to Christianity but didn't want to lose his Indian heritage in the process. He told his people, "We are going to follow the Bible but we're going to do it in a tee pee. We will build an alter out of earth and eat the peyote to cure our ills." This was the birth of the Native American Church.

"The NAC was finally chartered in 1918 near El Reno, Oklahoma" (Heart 198). It's organized primarily to pray for people in need. The following (found in Heart's book, *"The Wind is My Mother"*) is a sample of the NAC beliefs and practices:

---Meetings are held in a tee pee. The tee pee itself is

full of symbolism. Each pole comes from a different place just as people come from different places. The poles cross at the top symbolic of the cross of Christ. When the red flap is opened it symbolizes Christ spilling his blood for the people. When you enter the tee pee, you have to bend down to get through the door. The "bowing down" shows humility before God and man:

---Meetings are not held regularly but only when someone is in need:

---They don't necessarily believe in the tribunal godhead, but experience the joy of Christ' presence and talk directly to the Great Spirit of God:

---The tee pee meeting starts with lots of singing and fellowship. The part traditional Christianity would call "the Service," begins at midnight and last until sunrise. A practice taken from Genesis Chapter 1, "…this was the evening and morning of the …day":

---At midnight, the alter is swept clean, symbolizing you will start a new day "clean:"

---They sit in a circle symbolizing the eternal Circle of Life, which the Sacred Hoop represents:

---There is no "Leader" or "Preacher." All are equal. The one responsible for sitting up the tee pee is called the "Roadman" and the one responsible for starting and tending the fire is called the "Fireman:"

---Everyone is called "Brother" or "Sister." The elderly are called "Grandfather" or "Grandmother." Guest are called "Relatives," giving the NAC a real sense of family:

---Cedar wood is burned --- its smoke carries one's prayer up to the Creator:

---The Sacred Pipe plays a major role. Its care and use are sacred and complicated. One is expected "to know the rules for the Pipe before entering the tee pee." The Pipe is <u>not</u> a dope pipe and generally the tobacco used is not inhaled but "puffed." These puffs carry one's prayers and essence up and out the tee pee opening to the Great Spirit of God. Much like the "rule" for Communion or the Lord's Supper, (…examine yourself first…) clean yourself internally before smoking the Sacred Pipe. Taking it with unresolved anger or negative feelings will have negative results: "…for this many are weak and sickly and many sleep" I Corinthians 11:28-30). The smoke carries your essence up to God, so make sure your <u>clean</u> first:

---The alter is made of earth shaped like a hoof-print, in remembrance of Jesus riding into Jerusalem on a colt:

---The Round Gourd is shaken --- round like the Circle of Life. Its tassels are red, representing the shed blood of Jesus, the beginning and end of the Circle of Life:

---A staff is passed around. Bringing to memory how the Creator empowered Moses through the staff to guide His people. It's also a "walking stick," symbolizing how The Great Spirit walks with you on your journeys:

---The Kettle Drum has important symbolism. In Genesis Chapter 3, God covered Adam and Eve with animal skins …so water is poured into the drum and its covered with a skin. The skin is tied with cords crisscrossing on the bottom to make a "Star." The Star the wise men followed to baby Jesus. The "wise" will listen to the beat of the drum (The heartbeat of the Father) and follow the Star to find Jesus:

---Peyote was used until the 1990 Supreme Court prohibited its use, including in sacramental use. Later, in 1995, a bill was passed allowing the NAC to use peyote in its ritual healings (Heart 210).

The basic philosophy of the Native American Church is "where-ever you stand is the center of the universe --- God is the center so he surrounds you where-ever you stand." They use the analogy of the tree to fuse with Christianity: Each denomination is a limb, a branch, or a tiny twig on the greater tree --- The NAC is a twig and just as much a part of the tree as the larger denominations. All are attached to the tree and the tree is the Great Spirit of God.

The NAC does not print recruiting material; does not take tithes; does not send out missionaries and its Roadmen receive no paycheck. Its love for the Great Spirit of God and his Christ are practiced in ways of the Native Americans can relate to and draw nearer to God. (See Shamanism in INDEX).

Long before Europeans reached the Americas, Indians were already here. Although Christianity as an "organized religion" did not reach the American until the 14th century with explorers, and the NAC wasn't chartered until 1918, its people are the oldest on American soil, making them the oldest American part of our *Great American Stew*. Their traditions, Shaman, Medicine Men, symbolism and way of viewing the universe, are a part of our heritage. All this goes into our Stew and gives it an original American flavor found nowhere else in the world.

NAZARENE (Church of)

The Church of the Nazarenes emerged out of America's 19th century Wesleyan Holiness movement. The church, as we know it today, is a product of the merger of three separate denominations, who themselves are products of mergers of other denominations:

1) The Western" group was the Church of the Nazarene, founded in 1895, in Las Angeles by Phineas Bresee, a minister in the Methodist Episcopal Church.

2) The "Eastern" group was the Association of Pentecostal Churches of America, founded in 1897 through the merger of two other denominations: the Central Evangelical Holiness Association, and the Association of Pentecostal Churches of America.

3) The "Southern" group, mostly in Texas, was a merger of two groups: the Holiness Church of Christ and the Pentecostal Nazarene.

The official "founding date" of the merger into the Church of the Nazarene was October 1908. They agreed to keep the "Manual" (to become the *"Manual of the Church of the Nazarene"*) from the Eastern group, the title from the Western group, and the governing system of the Southern group. By 1922 some had pulled away to form the Wesleyan Church, but leaving the Church of the Nazarene as the largest of the two.

Over time many other groups have split from the main body to form their own denominations: Peoples Missionary Church (1912), Bible Missionary Church (1955), Wesleyan Holiness Association of Churches (1955), the Nazarene Baptist Church (1960), and the Fellowship of Charismatic Nazarenes (1972), just to name a few. The Church of the Nazarene grew to become internationally recognized and by 2001, 45% of its voting delegates were non-English speaking members.

The denominational name was first recommended (1895)by a former president of USC, Dr. Joseph P. Widery. The name came to him after spending the whole night in prayer. In the *New Testament*, Jesus was continually known as "the Nazarene," but as Gentile Christianity spread, the name became dismissed as the name of "Christ" became popularly used. In keeping with its philosophy (of "helping people") the Church adopted the name "Nazarene" as its title because it reflected Christ as a helper and a healer.

Like most large denominations, doctrine may vary somewhat from church to church, but its official teachings are pulled from its Manual. It holds sixteen *"Articles of Faith"* as their guide for Christian living:

Beliefs & Practices

---One eternal God manifest in a threefold nature:

---Two ritualized Sacraments are Baptism (by immersion, pouring, or sprinkling) and the Lords Supper to be taken no less than four times a year:

---The divinity of Jesus and the Holy Spirit:

---The Bible as the authorized word of God:

---The work of atonement:

---Original sin and personal sin:

---Prevenient Grace, Justifying Grace, and Sanctifying Grace. Good works are the Fruits of one's salvation:

---Need for repentance:

---Justification, regeneration and adoption:

---The Church is the Body of Christ:

---Infants can be dedicated by immersion with the understanding that it does not give them salvation:

---The return of Jesus as the Savior and King of Kings:

---Divine healing:

---Resurrection of the dead:

---They fall on the Arminianism side of the scale. Salvation is available to all who choose to accept saving grace:

---They do not believe Christians are helpless against sin, but that sin should be a rare exception in the daily life of a sanctified Christian (John Wesley's concept of "entire sanctification"):

---Justification through faith alone:

Historically, the Church was founded in order to help the poor. Alcohol, gambling, drugs and such are the addictions that keep people poor … so a Nazarene must abstain from these things in order to help others in their walk "with" or "toward" God. Their services are standard (Sunday mornings, evenings, and Wednesday nights) with old as well as contemporary music, prayer, special music, reading of scripture, sermon, offerings, and an alter call if needed.

Although it's a combination of Episcopal and Congregational style of organization, the Church of the Nazarene uses a form of representative government with power shared between the members and the clergy. Every 4 to 6 years qualified ordained elders are elected to one of six positions on the Board of General Superintendents. The Church of the Nazarene is one of the few denominations who have both, "ordained Elders" and "ordained Deacons."

Since its beginnings, this American found denomination is totally committed to helping others (Matthew 25), the "Great Commission," Missionary work, education, and instruction on the Christian Walk through such organizations as The Jesus Film Project (JFP), and Global Missions (GM).

Nazarenes are helpers, willing to help those in need. In this "helping attitude," they not only reflect Jesus but also reflect the concept of America as a helping nation. For this, the Church of the Nazarene has become a sweetener in our *Great Stew of Denominationalism*. They take the bitterness away and replace it with the sweet fruits of the Spirit. For this, we are grateful.

PENTECOSTAL

An exclusively American born denomination, the Pentecostal Church emerged out of the Holiness movement around the turn of the century. Their hinge-pen doctrine is the empowerment by the Holy Ghost as evidenced by the speaking in tongues after baptism of the Holy Ghost: (Acts 2:38). This lively denomination can be traced directly to two men: Charles Parham (1873-1929) and an African American, William Seymour (1870-1922).

Parham, the founder of Bethel Bible College in Topeka, Kansas, and Seymour, African American Holiness evangelist from Louisiana, were convinced that the gifts of the Holy Spirit, which had been demonstrated by the Apostles, are still available to Christians in modern times as well. The phenomenon called "Pentecostalism" is based on speaking in tongues and Pentecostalism began in America. The first official (modern) incident of speaking in tongues occurred in Topeka in 1901, when a young woman named Agnes Ozman, a student at Bethel College, spoke in tongues while at the campus Holiness Church of Parham (Rhodes 211). Three days later Parham himself spoke in tongues. He then moved to Texas where he opened a Pentecostal school in Houston.

There, in Houston, a Holiness minister named William Seymour, who had studied at Bethel and followed Parham to Texas, attended the school and helped promote the belief that "the Holy Ghost is evidenced in the believer by supernatural manifestations such as the speaking in tongues." Five years later, Seymour went to Los Angeles and led the famous Revival on Azusa Street from 1906 to 1908 (Rhodes 312).

It was there, on Azusa Street, participants experienced the baptism of the Holy Ghost (as Seymour & Parham had taught) and many were healed of illnesses while others spoke in tongues. People flocked to Azusa from all over the United States to witness and to experience this Holy Ghost Revival. Afterwards they carried the message back home, thus, not only was the Pentecostal Church born but its message was spread nationwide at the same time.

In time, a number of different Pentecostal Churches emerged: Pentecostal Holiness Church, Church of God in Christ, Church of God (Tennessee), Apostolic Faith (Oregon), Assemblies of God, Church of the Foursquare Gospel, and the Universal Pentecostal Church, just to name a few. In the 1960's, the Pentecostal experience began to penetrate some mainline churches and denominational lines, including the Catholic Church. This experience became known as the "Charismatic movement" (Rhodes 313) and was popularized in "How To Restore Spirituality" books. Out of this a completely new genre of literature was born. This included David Wilkerson's "*The Cross and the Switchblade,*" John Sherrill's "*They Spoke With Other Tongues,*" and thousands of other Charismatic books promoting the charisma (the personality) of the Holy Ghost.

Beliefs & Practices

In General, Pentecostal Churches are fundamental and evangelical. Even though beliefs may vary slightly from Church to Church, the central beliefs are pretty consistent across the board:

---Salvation is through the atoning blood of Christ:

---The virgin birth of Jesus is evidence of the deity of Jesus:

---The literal infallibility of the Scriptures:

---Most Pentecostals are "Pre-Millenniumist" (the rapture happens before the thousand year reign of Christ):

---Two sacraments are practiced...the "Lord's Super" and "Baptism by immersion, although some may observe foot washing and act out the feast days, but these are the exceptions not the rule:

---Pentecostals are Trinitarian but place greater emphasis on the direct action of the Holy Ghost:

---Most don't have to have the standard educational requirements for clergy but more important to them is evidence of the Spirit working in the preacher's life:

---The Holy Ghost is the witness of one's salvation in two ways---by inward Direct witness and guidance in the believer's life---and by outward evidence of the believer's exhibiting the gift of speaking in tongues:

---Music plays an important role in worship to help the congregation get "in the right mind-set" to hear and be filled with the Holy Ghost:

---Modest dress is preached and strictly practiced:

---When one walks into an Apostolic Service, (an extreme branch of the Pentecostal Movement) they will notice that, generally, women sit on one side and men on the other.

Pentecostal women are known for their hair being "up in a bun" and the modest manner of their dress. The worship service is filled with hymns and music, shouts of praise, hand waving throughout the service, and the message is that contemporary Christians can receive the same spiritual gifts that the New Testament Apostles received. Because of this message many Churches incorporate the word "Apostolic" into their Church name.

Pentecostalism took America by storm, surging to memberships well into the millions. For this as well as for its Apostolic message and its Charismatic contributions to main-line Churches, Pentecostalism has become a main ingredient in the *Great Denominational Stew*. It's to our *Stew* as "snap crackle and pop" is to Rice Crispies! It's the excitement, the music, and the joyfulness of Charismatic Christianity in America.

FOURSQUARE GOSPEL CHURCH

Although it's under the denominational umbrella of "Pentecostal," the Foursquare Gospel Church is such a phenomenal Church that it merits a special mention in this section. "Phenomenal" because it's one of only a handful of true Protestant Churches founded by a woman. A woman named Aimee Semple McPherson (1890-1944). This Church is a tribute to the organizing genius and striking methods of its founder" (Mead 292).

Born in Ontario in 1890, Aimee's mother was a member of the Salvation Army and dedicated Aimee to God at birth. The "Azusa Street Revival" which birthed Pentecostalism in America (occurred from 1906 to 1908) played a major role in Aimee's Christian development. At 17 years old (in 1907), she was converted and married a missionary named Robert Semple. Together they traveled as missionaries until he died of malaria in China in 1910.

"Back in the United States she married Harold McPherson and they began holding Pentecostal-style evangelistic meetings. After they divorced [remembering her mother's dedication] she continued on the work of evangelism" (Rhodes 330). Settling in Los Angeles in 1923, Aimee, along with supporters and lots of fund raising built the "Angeles Temple" in Los Angeles, which seated 5,300 people… one of the first Mega-Churches. With her children, Roberta and Rolf as well as many followers, she formed the Echo Park Evangelistic Association, The Lighthouse of International Foursquare Evangelism (the L.I.F.E.) Bible College, and the International Church of the Foursquare Gospel.

Aimee was not only blessed with outstanding speaking ability and faith in prayer, but used unconventional means (of the day) to communicate the gospel, including dramas, oratorios, and specially crafted messages. Her reoccurring theme was the "Foursquare Gospel" which was:

1) Christ as Savior.

2) Christ as Baptizer with the Holy Ghost.

3) Christ as Healer.

4) Christ the returning King.

Aimee would begin preaching in one corner of the sanctuary, preach on one of the topics above then move to another corner for the next topic…and so on until she had covered all four, completing the "Square" from which the denomination got its name: "Foursquare Gospel."

Although Pentecostal in practice and denomination, what sits Foursquare Gospel apart from the group is they focus almost entirely on Christ, whereas the general Pentecostal Churches focus mainly on gifts of the Holy Ghost. All believe in the trinity (God the Father, God the Son, and God the Holy Ghost) and that salvation is a work of grace received through faith in Jesus and not by any works.

The outstanding feature of the Foursquare is not in the doctrine or its practice---but is the people themselves. "They have no desire to compete or compare. They continually rejoice for every Body of believers which lifts the blood stained banner of Jesus Christ" (Foursquare 4). The tireless and devoted organizer, Aimee Semple McPherson, who was converted in the middle of the Azusa Street Revival and trained as a missionary, not only spread the Gospel of Christ but founded a Church, which lives out Jesus' command to "love one another."

Aimee McPherson is the flavor behind the sweet savor in our *Great Denominational Stew of Christianity*. The Foursquare Gospel Church adds health and nutrition to the dish and makes it a pleasure to not only taste but a pleasure to serve to those who hunger.

*(There is an excellent movie on Aimee's life titled, "*The Healer*," staring Elizabeth Taylor).

PRESBYTERIAN

The denominational title "Presbyterian" derives from the Greek word, "*presbuteros*," which means "elder" or in this case, "elder ruled." This is because Presbyterian Churches formed in the Protestant Reformation opposed Papal authority and were governed by elders called "Presbyters." This church is Protestant in practice, and is a product of the Congregationalist (Puritans) from the reformed tradition (Mead 124).

The story of the Reformed Churches, which includes Congregational and Presbyterian, among others, is the story of the Protestant reformation. Although their roots are in the Reformed Movement of Europe, Presbyterianism is ultimately the product of two men: John Calvin (1509-1564) and John Knox (1513-1572). "While Calvin did not found the Presbyterian Church, he certainly laid the foundation on which Presbyterianism emerged…he sought to establish a church government based on the New Testament concept of the offices of an elder. Though Calvin laid the ground-work the real founder was John Knox" (Rhodes 341).

Born in Scotland and ordained to the Roman Catholic priesthood in 1530, Knox converted to Protestantism around 1545, and became a thunderous and bold preacher. Quickly becoming a major force in the Reformed Church of Scotland, he was instrumental in it being recognized with its Presbyterian style government in 1567 (Rhodes 347). Soon Knox moved to England to preach and contribute to the *39 Articles of the Church of England.*

The *39 Articles* were important in stabilizing Protestantism but it wasn't enough. So out of the stormy political scene during the reign of England's Charles I, in 1643 the Parliament commissioned the Westminster Assembly to develop a creed (a Confession) for the Church of England. After a committee of 121 Puritan Ministers and over 1,000 sessions later the *Westminster Confession of Faith* was completed and would become the primary Confession of the Reformed Churches. Then in 1658, things changed for everyone! (See a copy in "Creeds").

That was the year Oliver Cromwell, a champion of Protestants, died---ending Puritan rule and England's status as a safe haven for Protestants (Walton 64). When Mary Tudor, a staunch Catholic, rose to power multitudes of Puritans, Reformed, Congregationalist, and Presbyterians exited Britain. "She [Mary] hated Protestants with everything in her, burning some 300 at the stake. No wonder she became known as Bloody Mary" (Rhodes 342).

Many Protestants fled to North America---the first Presbyterians association (a Presbytery") of local churches in America was founded in Philadelphia in 1706. In 1729 they officially adopted the *Westminster Confession of Faith* and settled down to the business of government and growth. The Presbyterian seed had been planted in New World soil and had taken root. It spread to touch every area of American life.

For example, "In the 1730's William Tennet Sr. (1673-1746) organized a 'Log College' in Neshaniny, Pennsylvania to train

Presbyterian Ministers. It grew to eventually become the College of New Jersey and later Princeton University" (Mead 129). Presbyterian evangelist were go-getters and started an emotional "new birth revivalism" in America. Their camp meetings and revivals played leading roles in the Great Awakening of the 1740's. Committed to God and to Country so earnestly that, for example, the President of Princeton, pastor John Witherspoon, (1727-94) was the only clergyman to sing the *Declaration of Independence.*

As with all denominations, over time there were splits and divisions in the ranks. The Old School Presbyterians held tightly to Calvinistic ideas while New School Presbyterians mainly in the north, placed more emphasis on colleges and social activism. Cumberland Presbyterians, Welsh and German Calvinist became American Presbyterians and brought their own cultures with them. By the 1920' to the 50's most had come together under the banner of the American (USA) Presbyterian Church.

Beliefs & Practices

The denomination grew healthy in unity even though there was not total unity in practice among the various Churches. Even in this absence of unity-in-practice the majority held, and still do, common beliefs and doctrines. It's what makes them Presbyterian:

> ---They believe the *Bible* is God's written Word and without error:

> ---The Trinity is God the Father, God the Son, and God the Holy Spirit: all three are One:

> ---Jesus was crucified for the sins of the "elect" (those chosen by God for salvation):

> ---Adam and Eve fell from original righteousness and all humans since have been born with a corrupted nature:

---Humanity cannot convert themselves so only those God Himself enables are elected to salvation: (See Calvinism in INDEX):

---They follow the TULIP of Calvinistic thought:

---The eternal invisible Church consist of all the elect, with Christ as its head---the earthly Church consist of all who profess faith in Jesus Christ and is governed by synods and councils:

---Women cannot become elders or any high rank in the Church itself:

---Baptism is by sprinkling or by pouring and infants as well as adults can partake of this sacrament, which is a sign of the engrafting into Christ:

---The Lord's supper is practiced regularly as a remembrance:

---The *Westminster Confession of Faith* is read and incorporated into Presbyterian thought:

---Eternal salvation is taught based on the TULIP doctrine of election--- when God elects one to salvation it cannot be undone:

---The total sovereignty of God is a core doctrine and God's will always over rides man's will:

---Pastors are selected by councils, with the advice of local elders held in high esteem.

The Presbyterian Church has been a rock of American Christianity. The image of the old conservative preacher has become a permanent fixture in our cultural heritage as a nation. Yes, Presbyterian Churches have had some recent conflicts and divisions over the role of women in the Church, same sex marriages, and even edited some parts of the *Confession,* but they will survive as most time-tested organizations do.

Presbyterianism is part of our past as well as our present. It is the thick rolling broth of our *Stew.* Old European, yet very American at the same time, gives it a strong flavor of familiarity…something old, yet new to the taste.

RASTAFARI (Rasta)

The Rastafarian movement, or rather "Rasta," is an Abrahamic movement that was popularized around 1930, in Jamaica. It's an eclectic mix of Christianity, Judaism, and Jamaican cultural traditions focused on a form of Emperor worship.

Its original followers worshipped the emperor of Ethiopia ("*Ra*" means "head" or "top one"). They saw the emperors as Prophets in an unbroken line of leaders from King Solomon to the present.

The "idea" has been around for a long time, but the Rastafarian style of spirituality flowed into the Christian culture of Jamaica in the 1930's. Much like the Native American's (Indians) blended their own traditions with Christianity, the Jamaicans blended Ethiopia emperor-worship, with Christianity and their own cultural traditions. In the late 20th century, the Rastafarian movement spread worldwide through popularization of Ragi singers such as Peter Tosh (1944-87) and Bob Marley (1945-81). Afrocentric quickly became a major player in American Christianity.

Rasta teaches that Ethiopia is "Zion" and all of Africa is the "Promised Land," if not "Heaven itself." There is an unbroken line of 225 Ethiopian emperors dating back to King Solomon to the present. The first was Menelik I, the son of Solomon and Queen of Sheba. From this, his son was an ancient Israelite, making all his descends Israelites as well. Out of this "line of thinking," came the concept of the "Black Jew:" since Solomon was black and a Jew, this made all his descendants Black Jews also…including Jesus. "Jesus was Black" became the cry of the Day!

In the "Back to Africa Movement" of the 1960'and 70's it became "Ok" to have pictures of a Black Jesus, Moses, Abraham, and of Black Angels. The Rasta doctrine was militant in appearance but peaceful in action. Rastafarian is a peaceful denomination that came out of a militant background. For example, the "dreadlocks" they wear were reminders of a legendary Ethiopian warrior named "Mau Mau" (spelling varies) who was captured and thrown into a cave/jail for years. His hair grew and he fashioned it into "pipes" (locks). He finally escaped and slaughtered all his oppressors. They "dreaded" to see his "locks" coming at them in war! Rasta wear dreadlocks as a reminder of his God-given strength.

They refer to God as "Jah," and pray to Him in their only two ceremonies: a "Reasoning," and a "Grounding."

A "**Reasoning**" Ceremony is a simple un-orchestrated event where cannabis ("Ganja") is gathered and smoked in a fellowship where they listen to "Jah" and reason out answers to common issues.

A "**Groundation**" is a Holy Day ceremony derived from the term *"Nya-binghi"* (*"Nya"* means "Black," and *"binghi"* is "victory"). Believed to have been used by an ancient order of black militants in eastern Africa that vowed to end oppression. The impromptu ceremony features lots of dancing, smoking *"ganja,"* and feasting. When one begins, the day is declared "Holy," and can last for days.

The Rasta is divided into many "Mansions" (sects and orders). The "Nyahbingh," the "Twelve Tribes of Israel," and the "Bobo Ashanti" (also called the "Bobo Dreads") are three of the most popular Mansions. The "Twelve Tribes of Israel," founded in 1968, by Dr. Vernon "Prophet" Gad, is considered the most liberal most influencal in America today. They say the Bible has been so corrupted by "those in power" that its only "half a book."

Once Rastafari was firmly established in America some rode the coat-tails of militant movements while others, the majority, chose to live peaceful lives and let "Jah" take care of oppression. Jesus and the Apostles are role models for a peaceful life. The following (taken mostly from Wikipedia) are a sample of common practices across the board:

Beliefs and Practices

---Monotheistic, worshiping a singular God called "Jah:"

---No trinity because Jah is a form of the Holy Spirit:

---Acknowledge Simon did witness to the Ethiopian Eunuch, but the Eunuch was already a follower of Jah so he was just being polite. Ethiopians knew about the Messiah long before Simon did:

---Western society is called "Babylon: Ethiopia" is "Zion:" and "Africa is "the Promised Land" if not actually "Heaven itself:"

---Immortalist, only a few from the lineage of Solomon will live forever in their own bodies:

---Baptism is not necessary, but is ok if you feel the need:

---Dreadlocks (on men or women) are not required but are preferred:

---Follow all food laws of the *Old Testament* unless nothing else is available. Jah provided it, so eat:

---The Cross-of-Jesus is revered because Jesus was a

great rebel against Rome and died on the Cross. It's a symbol of "giving your all for a cause." Jah lifted him up to heaven where He is the King of Kings:

---Reject materialism, oppression and cruelty to anyone:

---See themselves as "African Royalty," so they use titles such as "King, Prince, Queen, and Princess:"

---Jah speaks directly to them in the two ceremonies.

Agree with the Rastafarians or not --- follow their way of life or not --- Rasta is still an ingredient in our *Stew*. Its long history, its music, practices, and the Black Jesus have become an influential part of American culture and our *Great Stew of Denominationalism*.

SALVATION ARMY

While the Salvation Army is not a Methodist Church it did grow out of the Methodist concern for the impoverished people in England and has, in time, become a familiar institution in the United States. "The Salvation Army is neither a traditional denomination nor a traditional service organization, but a creative union of both" (Mead 229). Few realize that the Salvation Army is actually a denomination itself. It has become its own Church.

In 1868, a Methodist Minister in England named William Booth (1829-1912) left the Church to devote full time to evangelizing to the un-churched masses in London's seedy east end (Walton 83). He organized along the lines of a Methodist Mission and used the name "Christian Mission," but after realizing they were truly soldiers in a spiritual battle changed it to "The Salvation Army."

Under its new name, the Army grew past being just another social-help group and into its own being: an Army of Christian helpers and evangelists. Booth organized its dual function---a Church and a Social Agency---on a military format, which offered a helping hand to those in need but its first purpose was always salvation. The organization drew up its *"Articles of War"* and members were seen as soldiers: evangelists became officers, converts were called seekers, and Booth was designated as General.

The Army was and is designed to meet the needs of the whole person. The social services portion meets the needs of the poverty stricken, the neglected, the unwelcomed, those with physical/medical needs and in need of the necessities of daily life. It's a church with a heart as big as the world it serves!

Beliefs & Practices

Its fundamental doctrines are stated in the Eleven Cardinal Affirmations of its *"Foundation Deed"* (dated 1878). They believe and practice the following:

---The Bible is the only rule of Christian faith:

---They are basically Protestant in theology but not anti-Catholic in practice:

---They insist on modest dress and speech:

---They teach the Trinity of Father, Son and Holy Ghost:

---Sin is the destroyer of souls and society:

---Eternal hope is available only through Christ:

---Baptism is generally by immersion and for those who have accepted Jesus as Lord:

---The Lord's Supper is practiced as a remembrance and administrated often:

---Each Corps (Unit) is commanded by an officer who is responsible to the Divisional Headquarters:

---There are 40 Divisions in the USA in four territories:

---The Army is dispersed throughout the world in 109 countries, over one million active members in 140 languages:

---Basic training for each officer is two years in one of the Army's four schools:

---The national headquarters is in Alexandria, Virginia and holds high regard for citizen advisors and input of the general public.

The traditional military uniforms of the Salvation Army are familiar throughout the American cityscape. From bell ringing at mall doors at Christmas to the loving smile of the Homeless Shelter worker, the Army seems to be everywhere help is needed. They flavor our Great American *Stew* with true brotherly love and make sure it's served with a side dish of the Gospel and a smile.

UNITARIANS & UNIVERSALISTS

"Unitarianism and Universalism represent two quite distinct theological ideas that were brought together with the formation of the Unitarian Universalist Association of Congregations in 1961" (Mead 368). So before looking at the "Association" as it is today, it is necessary to go back and look at each of those two theological ideas before the merger.

Anti-Trinitarian, the basic tenet of **Unitarians** is that there is only one God, thus Jesus is not divine in essence. "While it claims to be a form of Christianity it denies the historical doctrines of the Christian Church: the Trinity, the virgin birth of Jesus, bodily resurrection, and the return of Christ" (Mead 504). Their history is often as hard to establish as their doctrine.

Claiming to reach back into the pre-fifth-century Christianity, Unitarianism, as we know it today actually began with the Protestant reformation among men such as Michel Servetus (1511-57) and Faustus Sucinus (1539-1604). Other honored persons in their history are Isaac Newton, John Lock, and John Melton, to name just a few (Mead 368).

Although the concept was from Europe, the Unitarian Church developed in New England's Congregational Churches being known as "Liberal Christian Churches." From 1805 to 1819 sermons were given by men such as Henry Ware (1764-1845) and William Channing (1780-1842) who were theologically, politically and socially, very liberal, if not outright radical! These sermons played a big part in reformation movements such as abolition, women's suffrage, and prison reform.

With influential members such as Susan B. Anthony, John and Abigail Adams, and Oliver Wendell Holmes, the Unitarian Congregationalist organized the Unitarian Association in 1825 with the goal of promoting the expansion of liberal religion. Independent Churches were ordered and grouped into thriving denominational unity across America. By 1961 there were 4 Unitarian Seminaries, 186 Churches, and well over 100,000 members. (See Unitarianism in INDEX for more).

As for the **Universalist**, "there are many forms of universalism, but in general, the term refers to the belief that all persons will be saved regardless of religious belief or non-belief" (Mead 369). They claim roots in early Christian Gnostics like Origen of Alexandria (185-259) and mystics such as Jacob Boehme (1722-78) of England who opposed the Calvinistic doctrine of the elect in his book *"The Union."* A Wesleyan evangelist in New Jersey named John Murray found groups of Universalist-minded people scattered throughout the East Coast and organized the first "Universalist Church in Gloucester, Massachusetts in 1779 (Mead 370). In 1790 a group met in Philadelphia and drafted their first *"Declaration of Faith."* It promoted pacifism, abolition of slavery, free public education and rejected the idea of eternal punishment in Hell for the lost.

By 1805, the American Universalist had, through trial and time, realized a consistent philosophy. It was reflected in the book, *"Treatise on Atonement"* by Hosea Ballea (1771-1851). The book was a rationalist rejection of eternal punishment in Hell, the Trinity, and the impossibility of miracles. It taught that God loved the human race as His very own children and that atonement for our sins are not found in any bloody sacrifice, but in the heroic example of Jesus who wanted to demonstrate God's love to all people.

Like their Unitarian brothers, the Universalist opposed slavery, stood for separation of Church and State, and maintained continued interest in the fields of science, civil rights, and other areas of social reform. "In May of 1961, the Unitarian and Universalist Churches in the USA and Canada were consolidated as the Unitarian Universalist Association of Congregations in North America (UUA) and has become one of the most influential liberal Church bodies in the entire world" (Mead 371).

Even though the two histories and beliefs are separate, the merger into the UUA brought unity and cohesion in beliefs. Some of these are:

Beliefs & Practices

---No one is required to subscribe to any particular religion or creed:

---Their main focus is on the human condition in relation to cultural diversity, feminist ideals, inner city ministries, gay and lesbian rights, and total separation of Church and State:

---A General Assembly is the overall policy-making body:

---Elected officers serve a four-year term:

---The UUA is headquartered in Boston and operated

its own publishing company ("Beacon Press") which produces fifty new titles each year.

The overall intent of the UUA is to have a positive effect on positive social change where one is free to choose his or her own course in accordance with what God has given them. This "positive attitude" has had a major influence on American thought and political evolution and has become part of our *Great American Stew*. Like it or not, it is that sweet and sour part of our Stew: some find it liking to their taste---while others find it sour and artificial.

WORLDWIDE CHURCH OF GOD (ARMSTRONGISM)

"The Worldwide Church of God has one of the most distinctive histories in American Christianity" (Mead 273). Originally known as "Radio City of God," the WCG officially began in 1933 under the leadership of Herbert W. Armstrong (1892-1986).

A Seventh Day Adventist who dabbled in the Church of the Latter Day Saints from time to time (Martin 304), Armstrong saw himself as a kind of Apostle sent to lead his Church into being the "Philadelphia Church of the Book of Revelation." A promoter of the Anglo-Israelite theory (Anglo-Saxons are the Lost ten tribes of Israel), early Armstrongist met in houses or private buildings rather than in Churches. His *"Plain Truth"* magazine reached a circulation of eight million copies a month, catapulting the WCG into the worldwide ministry with Churches in 100 countries.

The WCG, under its founder, Herbert Armstrong, had held to some traditional Christian teachings but also followed some distinctive theological ideas of their own:

> ---Armstrong did not accept the Holy Spirit as a distinctive person:

> ---He took a stand against bearing arms:

---Rejected the idea of an everlasting torment in Hell for the unsaved:

---Denied Christ' bodily resurrection:

---He introduced observation of the Passover of Jesus:

---The Sabbath was from Friday night to Saturday night:

---Forbidding the eating of unclean meats:

---Keeping the seven feast days:

---Taught non-participation in the holidays of Easter, Christmas, and Halloween:

The Church grew rapidly until the late 70's when Herbert's son, Garner Ted Armstrong, took over. He was "dis-fellowshipped" on four occasions for adultery (Mead 274) which finally resulted in a split in the WCG. A respected administrator named Joseph Tkach became Pastor General of the WCG and in 1937, Garner Ted founded the rival "Church of God International"---although it never numbered more than 5,000 and is still struggling after its founder's death in 2003.

In the 1980's Joseph Tkack stepped down and his son, Joseph Jr., took the helm. Under his leadership "the Church experienced nothing short of a religious conversion" (Mead 274). Many were disillusioned by the changes in attitude and practice Joseph Jr. brought to the Church following Armstrong's death and thousands left the WCG. A number of renegade groups formed to bring back (each in their own way) Armstrongism: the Philadelphia Church of God, the United Church of God, and the Restored Church of God.

Only the Philadelphia Church had more than 5,000 members. Founded in Edmond, Oklahoma, by Gerald Flurry, it now has around 100 Churches bearing the name. It holds strictly to Herbert Armstrong's original teachings, especially as outlined in his book, *"Mystery of the Ages."* For all intent and purposes, the Philadelphia Church is the incarnation of Herbert W. Armstrong's old World Wide Church of God.

Although somewhat changed from original Armstrongism, the current WCG still follows many of its traditional beliefs: salvation by grace and by the Law: denial of miracles: denial of the Holy Spirit as a person of the trinity: the keeping of the feast days as a requirement for salvation: and the ultimate end of salvation for man is to become a god oneself (Martin 317-323).

When viewing the WCG, on the surface it appears almost mainstream Baptist or Adventist…but upon a longer exposure it's clearly a unique denomination, complete with its own flavor. It stands out amid the denominations as flexible, somewhat chaotic, with old world as well as new world flavorings. But be careful of what you "think is real meat"…our *Stew* is full of imitation meat and fake vegetables. One needs a *Bible* to sort them out properly.

YAHWEH (House & Assembly)

Although the House of Yahweh (HOY) was "officially" founded in 1980 by Buffalo Bill Hawkins in Odessa, Texas, its conception goes back to a dream, a vision, he had back in 1951.

In the dream, called "The First Dream," Bill saw that he and his younger brother, J.G., were the Two Witnesses in Revelation Chapter 11. Their duty was four-fold: 1) To warn people of approaching end-time disasters: 2) To teach how traditional Christianity has been corrupted to the point of paganism: 3) To reinstate the observance of all the annual Feast Days and follow all commandments given to the ancient Israelites: 4) To teach the importance of using the "sacred" name of "Yahweh" rather than just "God."

A Sabbatarian, following a mix of Herbert Armstrong, Seventh

Day Adventist, and Messianic Judaism, Bill (through his Radio Talk Show) stressed the importance of keeping Saturday as the Seventh-day Sabbath; participation in all annual feast days; and using Hebrew names instead of the traditional English names in the Bible: "Yahweh" for God --- "Yahshua Messiah" for Jesus --- and all the titles of books in the Bible to be changed to their Hebrew names. All this was "nothing new" to American Christianity, but Bill's charismatic personality seemed to give it new life!

In 1969, the Hawkins Brothers, their families along with two other couples, moved to Israel. That same year an ancient door was unearthed. On its mantel was the Hebrew inscription, *"BAYIT YHWH"* (House of Yahweh). Bill took it as a sign --- a confirmation --- of his calling to revive Hebrew names to Christianity. Therefore, in the same manner as Muslims change their American names to Arabic names, the Hawkins changed their names to Hebrew names. Bill selected *"Yissrel,"* while his brother became *"Yaaqoh."*

Next came changing words they deemed as "pagan" to Hebrew, or at least to understandable English. The pagan word "Jesus" became *"Yahshua"* --- "Church" was pagan for "circle" used in pagan rituals so "House" became the accepted term --- "Congregation" was pagan so it was replaced with "Assembly" --- "Bible is pagan so "the Book" replaced it --- and even "Christ" was decidedly pagan and was replaced with *"Messiah"* --- and so on down the list...

In 1975, they moved back to the U.S.A., settling in Odessa, Texas, to lay the foundation for HOY. It was chartered in 1980 as "the House of Yahweh Odessa."

As the denomination grew, the brothers grew apart, disagreeing on several points. Yisreal insisted on "Yahweh" only, while Yaaqoh claimed "El" of "Elohim" was correct. They split into two groups. The older brother moved to Abilene and opened "the House of Yahweh Abilene," while the younger brother stayed in Odessa with "the House of Yahweh Odessa." (He later changed it to "the Assembly of Yahweh"). Each published their own version of "the Book:" *"the Book of Yahweh"* and *"the Word of Yahweh"*).

During this period, Yisreal changed his name again: this time to "Israel Hawkins." Although somewhat different, both Books changed all references to "LORD, God, All Mighty," etc., to *"Yahweh:"* all references to "Jesus" to *"Yahshua;"* and the title of "Christ" became *"Messiah."*

The doctrinal lines between the HOY and the AOY are blurred at times but crystal clear at others. The following (taken mostly from Wikipedia) is a sample of their shared beliefs:

Beliefs and Practices

---Use of Hebrew names for all books in the Word and for all major figures:

---Holding Saturday as the Seventh-day Sabbath, and like the Seventh Day Adventist, teach that going to church on Sunday is a sign of the Beast:

---"Angel" is a pagan term so it's replaced with "Messenger(s):"

---Like the Jehovah's Witnesses, they don't celebrate Christmas, Easter, or Birthdays, and don't allow any religious pictures, crosses, statues or icons in their homes:

---Both fall toward the extreme end of Calvinism in that Yahweh "chooses you for salvation." You don't choose Him:

---With a Universalist twist, if in this life you never "come to Him," you will in another life. All will be saved in the end:

---Like the Amish and Quakers, they shun the word "Preacher," so leaders are referred to as "Elders:"

---Baptism must be performed in "moving water." Upon baptism (by a Chosen Elder), one will receive the Holy Spirit:

---Much like the "United Pentecostals," the Holy Spirit is the creative force of Yahweh, not a personal Being:

---Believe in their "own" type of speaking in tongues and healing by touch:

---Yahshua (Jesus) in not divine himself but only became the Son of Yahweh after baptism by John at the river Jordan:

---Monotheistic in that there is One God … everyone else were simply teachers showing us "how" Yahweh wants us to live and to worship Him.

---Yahshua (Jesus) was the sacrificial Lamb of Yahweh so he is placed in a seat of honor at the right hand of Yahweh. All must come through him to get to Yahweh:

---An off shoot called "the Sanctuary of the House of Yahweh," insist all members make a pilgrimage to Abilene three times a year to observe Passover, Pentecost, and Tabernacles:

---After J.G. died, Israel Hawkins is the last True Prophet. To ignore him is to ignore Yahweh's words and instructions.

Israel Hawkins has written dozens of books: "The Two Witnesses," "Deception," "The Mark of The Beast," and "Satan Unveiled," to name a few. After dozens of failed prophecies such as "4/5's of humans in the world will be wiped out by 2003; Nuclear war will break out on September 12, 2006;" (in October of 2006, this date was moved up to "June 12, 2008;") and so on. These "type" of prophecies have earned Israel Hawkins a place along with the other self-proclaimed prophet such as Jim Jones, David Koresh, and H.W. Armstrong. Naturally, only members of the "Yahweh" groups will go to Heaven as Priest and Kings. Everyone else, based on their works, will be servants to these "Kings."

Like it or not, the Yahwehist are a part of our Stew: listed right there in the ingredients. It's odd paradigm on Christianity puts it in a class of its own but does not push it out of America. It was founded in America…by an American, and teaches to Americans. One is free to "scoop it up" or "pass it up!" It's in the Stew and the choice is yours to make.

XIII.

<u>NEW AGERS & THE JESUS MOVEMENT</u>

"In the last decades [of the 20th century] there has been an upsurge in the number of religious groups actively seeking a following" (Scotland 5). Religion itself is a difficult word to define but its effect is universal. It brings people together, binds them together in beliefs, in practice, in values, morals, and in tradition. All religions behave like a living organism. And like all living organism, religious groups expend energy, expand and contract, spread out, mutate and divide into new yet similar organisms. This social organism is, in this case, called a "Movement" and Christianity in the United States experienced just such a powerful movement which came to be called the "New Age." (Currently called "The Emerging Church movement").

All organisms, especially social ones, are ultimately the collective product of three elements:

1) The organism's genetic inheritance…where it came from

2) What the organism takes into its body …"we are what we eat."

3) It's a product of its environment: the environment determines its health, movement limitations, and its life's duration.

The New Age Movement is no exception. Its alive through its followers. Through them it has defined needs and survival instincts. It breathes, moves, communicates, reproduces and under the right circumstances it can die out…as many other movements, religions, denominations and philosophies have.

The first element is Genetic Inheritance. The New Age is not a Church but is a powerful movement consisting of tens of thousands of different people, all moving in the same philosophical and theological direction. It takes its name from the "Age of Aquarius" which is the "New Age" we are living in according to those who dabble in such things. Its followers, mostly Baby Boomers, were dissatisfied with the establishment, mainstream Christianity, and our materialistic society. They were united---drawn together---by music, art, literature, and the desire to express themselves in a new and less restricted way. They strived to express their religious beliefs under the banner of purity and unconditional love. In a broad sense these antiestablishment New Agers seeking a pure love, a pure truth, pure freedom and a pure worship were the next generation of Puritans.

Drawing from the Hippy Culture and the Jesus Movement (often called "Jesus Freaks") they saw the Christian Church of their fathers as corrupted. They saw governments as oppressive. They saw economic classes skewed to favor the rich. They rebelled against the ring tradition had placed in their nose and set out to change the world…change their world by "striving to reach one's higher self" which will result in the capacity to express unconditional love" (Scotland 213). Thus, the social makeup---the genetic inheritance---of the New Ages consisted of people who want change: freedom to express love, which will lead them to a better life and make a better land to live in. As John Lennon might sing, "Imagine all the people…Imagine such a world…"

The second element of the organism is "what it takes into its system to function and to survive." The social unrest and dissatisfaction with America's materialistic society drove these rebels straight into the open jaws of the movement. They, their energy, their dreams, their youthful lust and thirst for self-expression became the fuel which powered the New Age. The philosophies of these Baby Boomers became part of the organism itself. "We are what we eat!" The result was that the New Age reflected in their music, their art, their ideals, their ideas about who God is and their role in the grand scheme of things. It was all digested and absorbed to become the collective being of the "New Age" itself: the "Age of Aquarius."

The down side is that all organisms emit waste. In this case the waste emitted by the New Agers was the destructive effects of drugs (mostly meth, LSD, heroin, and mushrooms) occultism and spiritualism (ghost chasing by any other name) and the non-productive lives which resulted from the nothing-ness of eastern mysticism. Their ideology of free love lead to rampant outbreaks of sexually transmitted diseases and America's first surge of illegitimate births, especially among teenagers.

The third element of an organism is "the organism is a product of its environment." The mid 20th century was a time of change. The economic boundaries were changing. Class structures was changing. Concepts of war were changing. People were leaving their family farms and moving to factory jobs in the big cities. The 60's were a transition time between established traditions and what was to be. And the Baby Boomers---the life force of the organism---landed right in the middle of it.

"It" is the flood of Eastern religions, Transcendentalism, new Spiritualism, Shamanism, Wicca, LeVey's Church of Satan, Yoga, Astrology, esoteric healing, Crystal Power, Tarot readings, Sum Myan Moon's "Unification Church," UFO cults and the New and Improved Theosophy. "It" all converged on the fertile minds of the New Agers: the ones searching for self- expression found exactly what they were looking for!

Out of this mix, this buffet of religious concepts, the Movement (like all living organisms) had offspring. Offspring, which carried the parent's genes but were different enough to be their "own" individual beings. Like it or not, the 60's with all its turmoil, rebellion, flower power and new way of looking at life, is a permanent part of the American psyche. "It" effected every offspring of the American experience, including Christianity. One such offspring of the Age of Aquarius and the Jesus Movement was the hippie Christian denomination called "The Children of God" (COG).

CHILDREN OF GOD (The Family)

"The roots of the Children of God, as they were originally known, lie in the counterculture youth movement of the 1960's, which spawned groups of flower children, anti-war protesters, and pot smoking back packers (Scotland 84). The founder of COG, a California native, was David Berg (1919-94). He was born into a Christian home where his Father was a Missionary Alliance Pastor and his Mother a radio evangelist.

As an adult, Berg married his first wife, Janet Miller in 1943 (she later became known as "Mother Eve"). Berg became a pastor himself in Arizona and traveled the USA with Fred Jordan pioneering televangelism. Eventually founding a Christian commune in Texas called "Soul Clinic Ranch." Later he joined the Assemblies of God and in 1967 became a leader of the "Teen Challenge" program out of Huntington Beach, California (Scotland 85).

Having great charisma and influence with the hippie culture of the times, he attracted them by the busloads! Eventually separating from all mainline denominations and starting his own called the "Light Club," with the followers called "Light Clubbers." These "Clubbers" were more than eager to share in Berg's vision and hip-teachings about Christianity. Communal lifestyles, free love, "natural" drugs and painted buses became their trademark. Berg became a legend in his own time---but often, living legends tend to fall---and fall he did!

Like so many other "Pop" leaders, he began having wild visions, prophesies, and spiritual visits. By 1969 (a very active year in cult activities), after having a vision about California being destroyed by an earthquake, he ordered the "Family" to move immediately. They packed up and wandered throughout the Southwest in caravans of brightly painted buses, vans and gypsy type campers. It was during this migration period that they picked up the name "Flower Children," but Berg changed it to "Children of God." In no time at all their "earned reputation" as hippies, vagabonds, and panhandles caused them more than one run in with the law. Their lifestyle of music, open expression, and communal living, attracted the minds and curiosity of thousands of America's youth. It was love, love, love, on the surface, but something all together different within the group itself.

In 1972, Berg announced that he was "Moses David the last prophet of God." He wrote letters and essays known as "Mo Letters," and instructed his followers to do what he called "Litnessing." That is, going out on the streets and offering his "Mo Letters" for donations. (The practice of today's mega Televangelist offering their 'books for donations" and "Partnerships for donations" is no different). Berg took the practice of Litnessing to a whole new level when he insisted that female members engage in what he called "Flirty Fishing." Based on the phrase "Fisher of men," Berg insisted that female Family members were to go to clubs, restaurants, and street corners wearing mini-skirts and alluring low-cut tops to "encourage" men toward a commitment to Christ. They were also "encouraged" to "go all the way" if the donation for the Family was sufficient. In his 1979 report Berg called them "hookers for Jesus" and bragged that "they had witnessed in this way to over a quarter million souls" (Scotland 87). This concept has evolved but is still with many believers today in the form of what is called "Missionary dating." This includes dating the unbeliever and being his boyfriend or girlfriend and hopefully, through the power of love, you will lead him (or her) to Jesus. This is very dangerous!

The Family grew and spread out internationally with 70 colonies in various parts of the world It reached its zenith in the early 1980's but the damage to traditional Christianity had already been done. Youth wanted self-expression and Free-Love-Christianity. The seed of free love, easy sex, ("only if you love them though") drugs ("only if their natural") and an "if it feels good do it" (because God made everything good) attitude toward life had already taken root in a generation who would pass it on to future generations who would call it "Liberal Christianity."

The denomination of the Children of God is still around and avoids the old title of "the Family." Their headquarters is now in Lechesteshire, England, and is presided over by an ex-Salvation Army band leader named Gideon Scott and his wife Rachel. The legacy of the COG is still with American Christianity in the easy believe-ism Churches, which are, once again, filling with dissatisfied youths looking for self-expression and a quick fix of Jesus.

When you go into a modern church and see a spiked-haired youth sporting piercings, tacks, and dressed in rebellious clothing while screaming out contemporary Christian rock lyrics to overly-loud music, you are looking at the offspring of the Jesus Movement, Children of God, New Age, and Liberal "come as you are Christianity." The next generation of the Jesus Movement and the Family have arrived! The organism lives on…on American soil…

XIV

<u>CONCLUSION</u>

Well, here we are, at the beginning years of the 21st century. We've had over two thousand years to tamper with the Church Jesus built. We've changed it---no doubt about that. But have we changed it too much? How much is too much anyway?

Look at it this way: if you are given a red car and repaint it blue, you've changed it…but only its color. It's still the same car serving the same purpose it was designed for. But if you disregard the Owner's Manual and change tire sizes, tint the windows, install a sunroof, bigger speakers and softer seats, you've altered it into a different vehicle. You have redesigned it to fit "your personal taste and comfort." Even though it still drives like a car and handles pretty well, it now serves the purpose of its new designer: "You."

We have changed a lot of things in God's earthly Church… added a lot of features (sound systems, stained glass windows, Welch's Grape Juice, monthly partnerships, denominationalism, female Pastors and Bishops and so on) and even taken away many parts. But have we changed it into something else and only kept the name "Church?" Have we become the Designer of God's Church in America? Would Jesus recognize our *Denominational Stew* as His own recipe?

There are more denominations in America today than can be

discussed in this book: Waco's Branch Davidians, Hubbard's Church of Scientology, the Rosecoutians, Warren's Saddleback Church, Heaven's Gate, the Moonies, and T. D. Jakes, Potter's House in Dallas, Texas…just to name a few. Each one has, like all denominations and non-denominations have, altered the Church somewhat---changed it some---to suite their own interpretations, theological concepts and cultural biases. Simply put: they did what they thought was the right thing to do at the time.

As this book has shown through the evolution of American Denominations, "change" is just what mankind does. We change things. Whereas God took nothing and changed it into everything, we take something and change it into something else. Eve knew the order God had created in the Garden, yet she (by exercising her free will) desired to change it a little:

> "…she took of the fruit and did eat [the change] and gave also unto her Husband [get others involved] with her and he did eat." (Genesis 3:6)

Change seems to be a compulsion with us! Cain changed his offering from meat to grain…and later with the building of the Tower of Babel Nimrod tried to change the path to Heaven from that of faith to that of works (see Genesis chapter 11). When we change one or more of the parameters of God's design it always brings negative consequences with it.

<u>First</u>, it effects the "changer." Adam and Eve lost Paradise: Sampson lost his freedom: Jezebel her life: Judas everything: and more currently, David Koresh lost his life: Tammy Fay Baker lost her reputation: and many Pastors have lost entire congregations!

<u>Secondly</u>, change negatively "affects those around the Changer" (including future generations). For example, the incestuous acts of Lot's two daughters in Genesis 19:32-38 spawned the nations of the Moabites and the Ammonites who became deadly enemies of Israel. Aaron's golden calf in Exodus 32 (and later "doubting God's

protective power) cost the Israelites forty years in the wilderness. And more contemporarily, the Great Disappointment" of the early Millerites (see "Adventist") cost many their faith all together. General curses are very real, very deadly, and still exist today.

Thirdly, the Changer will be "separated from God." Not totally, but will be distanced from God and will suffer His anger. Adam and Eve were driven from the Garden and from His presence (Genesis 3:24). Cain went from the presence of the LORD (Genesis 4:16). Moses was held back from entering the Promised Land, and so on throughout the *Bible*. The point is that changing the way God establishes something (including His Son's earthly Churches) is a very serious matter.

Serious because it usurps God's authority. Changing His established order is an attempt to put oneself in God's place. And we all know what happened to Lucifer when he tried that (see Isaiah 14:12015 & Ezekiel 28:11-19). He got his name changed and was forced to move. "...he was cast out into the earth..." (Revelation 12:9). "Remember, it's all spiritual warfare. It's just taking place on earth now" (Boyd 5). Paul knew this when he penned Ephesians 6:12...

> "For we wrestle not against flesh and blood, but against principalities, against powers, against the rulers of darkness of this world, against spiritual wickedness in high places."

Also in II Corinthians 11...

> 13. ...for such are false apostles, deceitful workers, transforming Themselves into the apostles of Christ.

> 14. And marvel not: for Satan himself is transformed into an angel of light.

> 15. Therefore it is no great thing if his ministers also be transformed Into ministers of righteousness.

So with this in mind---that it's all spiritual warfare and not all Churches are really "of" God---how can we, as followers of Christ, discern Truth from deception when looking for a Church home? The place to start is to read your Bible constantly. Many good men died so that you could have that Bible. Mark Twain once said:

> "A man who can read but chooses not to, is no different than a man who can't read at all!"

And in the same light, I say:

> **"A man who has a Bible and doesn't read it, is no different than a man who doesn't have a Bible at all!"**

Do as Paul instructed in II Timothy 2:15 and "study" the word of God. Learn to rightly "divide" it. To learn what goes with what and why. It's all about TRUTH and we're in a war over Truth. (I highly recommend John McAuthor's book titled, "***The Truth War***"). In I John 4:1 we are instructed to "try [test] the spirits…" Don't blindly accept any religious speech just because it sounds good, quotes some verses and uses a lot of Holy names. Lay it beside what God says. Is it Truth? See if it matches with His version of Truth. We can't do this unless we "read" the Bible ourselves.

When visiting a Church it's a good rule-of-thumb to check out the three C's: Content, Conduct, and Converts. Armed with scriptural knowledge and guided by the true Spirit of God, look for the "three C's."

Content: when visiting a Church resist the urge to get carried away with the programs, the music, and the flow of it all. Pay attention to the Church's content---its message---what its all about there. It should reflect aspects of Jesus…lifting Him up. We know from John 14:6 that Jesus "is the truth," and I Timothy 3:15 tells us that "the Church is the pillar of the truth." The content of the Church should show this. It's not about lifting up the Pastor or the

Denomination as the pillar of truth. The Church itself is the pillar and its job is to hold Jesus up high for all to see and to worship.

Conduct: the conduct of the Church as a whole. Does it exhibit a genuine love or are they just going through the motions? He commanded us in John13:34 to "Love one another as I have loved you…" (and He loved us to the death). Scolding someone about "that's my parking space," or "that's where I always sit," gossiping and snubbing a stranger, is not showing much love is it? The next verse (verse 35) tells us "why" Jesus commanded us to love each other; "By this all men know ye are my disciples…" Look at the conduct of the Church with eyes wide open. See if it is producing disciples of the Denomination, disciples of the Pastor, disciples of the local Church, or is it producing genuine love filled disciples of Jesus Christ the Living God.

Converts: seek out and get to know the new converts. It's said that "you can tell the condition of a country by the smiles of its children." The same hold true for Church…"you can tell the condition of a Church by the smiles of its new converts…it's new babes in Christ." Let them tell you about the Church.

Why the new converts? Because the old-timers will tell you about the programs, the Churches history, who's who in Church circles, Church politics and so on. But the new converts should still be on fire for the Lord! They will eagerly tell you about Jesus and how they came to know Him. They should be filled with joy and zeal for the Lord. If not, then it's time to move on…

Lastly, read Chapter 2 & 3 of the book of Revelation. Its Jesus telling John about the seven Churches in Asia. By Him telling John He is also instructing us today on what a good Church is and isn't. In fact, a sizeable portion of the New Testament is about what a Church should be like. Romans, Corinthians, Galatians, Ephesians, Philippians, Colossians, the Thessalonians and even Hebrews are all written to or about Churches. It was written by God's Holy Spirit---it is written "to us." It is our guide and standard on the subject of Churches.

Don't be mislead by any other book or self-proclaimed "preacher of righteousness. Too many Christians are forgetting the truth [that the devil is still active in our churches]…they regard the emotional weight of the experience to be more truthful than the Word of God" (Weber 101). When visiting a Church look for and "expect truth" rather than searching for an emotional high.

Our Great American *Denominational Stew* is a part of us now (we are what we eat). As I've shown, parts of it are good and some not so good---some are healthy and some deadly---some lead straight to the Cross-while other parts lead to destruction. It's up to the disciples, the true followers of Christ, to decide which parts of the *Stew* he or she is willing to partake of. It's out there: the mysteries of the Gnostics: the ghostly deceptions of the New Agers; the charm of Deism: the love of the Monrovians: the faith of the Martyrs: the marketing techniques of the Mega-Churches and the Medicine Shows of the Televangelist. It's all for us to pick and choose from.

So let the Holy Spirit of God be your Guide and Wisdom your compass. The Great American Denominational Stew is ready to be served…invite Jesus to dine with you and dig in…

Bon Apetite! May God Bless you on your journey…

lms

References

Baxtor, Batsell Barton, *What Is the Church of Christ?* Hauin Publishing Co., Pasadena, TX

Berry, Harold J., *Examining the Cults: In Pursuit of Truth* (2004), Good News Broadcasting Association, Inc., (Back To the Bible Ministry), Lincoln, Nebraska

Boyd, Gregory A., the *God War* (1997), Inter-Varsity Press, Downers Grove, IL

Chapel Library, *The Choice…Man's Or God's*, a ministry of Mt. Zion Bible Church, Chapel Library Publications, Pensacola, FL

Eerdman's Bible Dictionary (1987), edited by Allen C. Myers, Eerdman's Publishing Co., Grand Rapids, MI

Foursquare, *What the Foursquare Believes* (2006), Published by the International Church of Foursquare Gospel, Los Angeles, CA

Foxe, John, *Foxes Book of Martyrs*, 11th reprint (2006) originally titled *"The Acts and Monuments of the Church,"* Fleming R. Revell and Baker Publishing Group, Grand Rapids, MI

Funk & Wagnall's New Encyclopedia ((1996), Funk & Wagnall Inc. and Donnelley & Sons Co., USA

Gallagher, Steve, *Deny Yourself* (2000), Pure Life Ministries and Dry Ridge Kentucky/Chapel Library and Publishing, Pensacola, FL

Grudem, Wayne, *Systematic Theology* (2000), Inter-Varsity Press, Leicester England & Zondervon

Heart, Bear, *The Wind is My Mother: The life & teachings of a Native American Shaman*. Berkley Publishing Group, New York, NY

Heilbrener, Robert L., the *Worldly Philosophers, Rev, Ed.* (1961), Simon & Schuster, N.Y., NY

Hunt, David, *The Berean Call* (November 2006), Article in reprint from *"Occult Invasion: the Seduction of the World and the Church,"* also by David Hunt, PO Box 7019, Bend, OR

King James Version of the *Holy Bible* (1998), Thomas Nelson Publishing Co., Nashville, TN

LaTourette, Kenneth Scott, *History of Christianity: Reformation to the Present Vol. 2* (1975), Harper & Row Publishers, N.Y., NY

Martin, Walter, *Kingdom of the Cults, Limited Ed.* (1996), Bethany Publishing, Minneapolis, MI

McArthur, John Jr., *Charismatic Chaos* (1991), Zondervon Publishing Co., Grand Rapids, MI

Mead, Frank S., *Handbook of Denominations in the United States, 12Ed.* (2005), Abingdon Press, Nashville, TN

Murrell, Stanford E., *A Glorious Institution: The Church in History, Pt. 3 of 4* (1998), Mount Zion Publishing, Pensacola, FL

Nelson's New Illustrated Bible Dictionary (1999), Thomas Nelson Publishing, Nashville, TN

Office of the General Secretary, *History of the Wesleyan Church,* (2004), the Wesleyan Church Press, Indianapolis, IN

Peters, Peter J., *A Bible Story* (2003), Scriptures for America World Wide, La Porte, CA

Random House Webster's Dictionary 3rd Ed. (1998), Edited by Carol G. Graham, Ballantine Books, N.Y., NY

Rhodes, Ron, *the Complete Guide to Christian Denominations* (2005), Harvest House Publishers, Eugene, OR

Rod & Staff Publishers, *The Mennonites,* Crocket, KY (Given out by Grandview Fellowship, Pastor Marlin Kreider, Grandview, TX

Rose Publishing, (Pamphlet) *Christian History & Time Line* (1998), Rose Publishing Inc., Torrance, CA

Scotland, Nigel, *The Baker Pocket Guide to New Religions* (2006), published in the United States by Baker Publishing, Grand Rapids, MI

Shelly, Bruce L., *Church History: In Plain Language 2nd Ed.* (1995), Word Publishing & Thomas Nelson Publishing, Nashville, TN

Showater, Richard A., the *Conservative Mennonite Conference: A Short History* (1971), Conservative Mennonite Board of Missions, Irwin, OH

Truth Wars, the (2007), John McArthur, Thomas Nelson Publishing, Nashville, TN

Watson, Edward C., *(Weekly Magazine)* March 16, 2007 issue, the Week Publishers LLC, N.Y., NY

Weber, Stu, *Spirit Warriors*, Multnomah Publishers Inc., Sisters, OR

Wharton, Edward C., *the Church of Christ* (1977), Gospel Advocate Co., Nashville, TN

Creeds, Articles & Confessions

Apostles' Creed

Tradition has it that the Creed was written 10 days after Christ's ascension into Heaven but history tells a different story. The earliest documents found which hold this Creed is in the *Interrogatory Creed of Hippolytus* (A.D. 215). The Creed became the standard doctrine (teaching) for baptismal candidates at the Church of Rome. Below is the Traditional English Version:

> *I believe in God the Father, Maker of heaven and earth.*
>
> *And in Jesus Christ his only Son, our Lord; who was conceived by the Holy Ghost, born of the Virgin Mary, suffered under Pontius Pilate, was crucified, died, and rose from the; he ascended into heaven, and sitteth on the right hand of God the Father, Almighty; from thence he shall come to judge the quick and the dead.*
>
> *I believe in the Holy Ghost; the holy Catholic Church; the communion of the saints; the forgiveness of sins; the resurrection of the body; and life everlasting. AMEN.*

Nicene Creed (A.D. 325)

The Nicene convened in A.D. 325 to settle, among other issues, a problem regarding the nature of Christ. Out of it came this Creed:

> *I believe in one God the Father Almighty, Maker of heaven and earth, and of all things visible and invisible.*
>
> *And in one Lord Jesus Christ, the only begotten Son of God, begotten of the Father before all worlds, Light of Light, very God of very God, begotten, not made, being of one substance (essence) with the Father; by whom all things*

were made; who, for us men and for our salvation, came down from heaven, and was incarnate by the Holy Ghost of the Virgin Mary, and was made man; and was crucified also for us under Pontius Pilate; He suffered and was buried; and the third day He rose again, according to the Scriptures; and ascended into heaven, and sitteth on the right hand of Father, and shall come again, with glory, to judge both the quick and the dead, whose kingdom shall have no end.

And I believe in the Holy Ghost, the Lord and Giver of Life; who proceedeth from the Father; who with the Father and the Son together is worshipped and glorified; who spake by the Prophets. And I believe in one Holy Catholic and Apostolic Church. I acknowledge one baptism for the remission of sins; and I look for the resurrection of the dead, and the life of the world to come. Amen.

NOTE: this last paragraph was added in A.D. 381.

Articles of Faith

First established in 1563, the *Thirty Nine Articles of Faith* (the *XXXIX Articles*) served to define the doctrine of the Church of England's boundaries between the Calvinist doctrine and that of the Roman Catholic Church. Prior to the death of King Henry (in 1547), many positional articles were published: the *Ten Articles* in 1536: the *Six Articles* in 1539 (which was pro-Catholic): the *King's Book* in 1543: and the *Forty Two Articles* in 1552. Finally, during the reign of Elizabeth I the *Thirty Nine Articles* was established in 1563 and finalized as the official doctrine of the Church of England in 1571.

Ten Articles of Faith (1536)

Published in 1536 by Thomas Cranmer, they were the first guidelines of the Church of England. The following is a summary of what each article addresses:

1) The binding authority of the Bible, the three ecumenical creeds, and the first four ecumenical councils.

2) The necessity of baptism for salvation, even in the case of infants…Article II proclaims that "infants ought to be baptized; that dying in infancy, they shall undoubtedly be saved thereby, and else not; that the opinions of Anabaptist and Pelagians are detestable heresies, and utterly to be condemned."

3) The sacrament of penance, with confession and absolution, are declared "expedient and necessary…"

4) The substantial, real, corporal presence of Christ' body and blood under the form of bread and wine in the Eucharist.

5) Justification by faith, joined with charity and obedience.

6) The use of images in churches.

7) The honoring of saints and the Virgin Mary.

8) The invocation of saints.

9) The observance of various rites and ceremonies as good and laudable, such as clerical vestments, sprinkling of holy water, bearing of candles on Candlemas Day, and giving of ashes on Ash Wednesday.

10) The doctrine of purgatory and prayers for the dead in purgatory…made purgatory a non-essential doctrine.

Bishops' Book (1537)

Written by forty-six "Divines," (eight were archbishops and seventeen were Doctors of Divinity, some which would later be involved in translating the *Bible* and compiling the *Prayer Book*), headed by Thomas Cranmer, this Book became the official doctrine of separation between the Church of England and the Roman

Church. It was later replaced by other creed but its impact was that of categorizing the new Anglican faith in England. Its theological position would evolve into the King's Book whose function was to educate the people in church doctrine and promote church unity.

Six Articles of Faith (1539)

In reaction to issues with the German Protestant King, Henry gave the "go ahead" to a committee to document the Church's position on what the Germans called "abuses allowed by the Anglican Church." On April 28, 1539, Parliament met for the first time in three years. One month later, in May, the House of Lords created a committee to examine and determine doctrine. They narrowed it down to six doctrinal issues:

1) Transubstantiation.

2) The reasonableness of withholding of the cup from the laity during communion.

3) Deals with Clerical celibacy.

4) Observance of vows of chastity.

5) Permission for private masses.

6) The importance of auricular confession.

Their position was pro-Catholic and after much heated debate finally passed Parliament. After Henry's death it was repealed by his son, Edward VI but continued to be a source of heated debate.

King's Book (1543)

The Necessary Doctrine and Erudition for Any Christian Man, also known as *The King's Book* because it was attributed to Henry VIII. Protestant in substance, it defined transubstantiation and the Six Articles of Faith, encouraged preaching and attacked the use of images. It became the standard of the day in the ongoing battle between separation of the Church of England and the Church of Rome.

Forty Two Articles of Faith (1552)

Completed in 1552, under the reign of Edward VI, they were intended to summarize Anglican doctrine as it existed under Edward VI who favored a more Protestant view. But with the Coronation of Mary I and the reunion of the Church of England and the Church of Rome, the Articles were never enforced. However, after the death of Mary they became the basis of the *Thirty Nine Articles of Faith.*

Convocation met, under Archbishop Parker in 1563 and revised the 43 down to 39. Elizabeth I reduced the number on down to 38 by throwing out Article XXIX; "the wicked do not eat the body of Christ." After she was excommunicated in 1570, the article was re-inserted by bishops, bringing its number back to "XXXIX."

Thirty Nine Articles of Faith (1563)

Not intended as a complete statement of the Christian faith, but only of the position of the Church of England in relation to the Church of Rome. The Articles argue against positions such as "the holding of goods in common" and "the necessity of believer's baptism." They were intended to incorporate a blend of theology and doctrine which would allow men to appeal to (in the broadest sense) domestic opinion. It opened a **via media**, or "middle path," between beliefs, traditions and practices of the Roman Church and those of the English Puritans.

The XXXIX is divided, in compliance with orders of Elizabeth I, into four sections:

Articles 1-8 deal with the "Catholic faith." The first five put forth statements concerning the nature of God in the Trinity. Articles 6 and 7 deal with scripture, and Article 8 discusses the essential creeds.

Articles 9-18 confront "personal liberty."

Within these Articles are topics of sin, justification, and the question of "eternal disposition of the soul." Much room is devoted to the Reformation doctrine of "justification by faith," closing with the topic of "good works are an outgrowth of faith and there is a role for the church and for sacraments."

Articles 19-31 explain "corporate Religion." It focuses extensively on the expression of faith in the public realm, the institutional church, councils, worship, ministry, and sacramental theology.

Articles 32-39 hold the miscellaneous items that dangled far too long by themselves. Items such as the Bishop of Rome has no jurisdiction in England.

Charles I of England, could be called "the first royal legalist" when in 1628 he issued a Royal Decree threatening action to be taken against anyone teaching personal interpretations or encouraging debate about them: "…no man hereafter shall either print or preach, to draw the Article aside any way, but shall submit to it in the plain and full meaning thereof: and shall not put his own sense or comment to the meaning of the Article, but shall take it in the literal and grammatical sense."

Although the Evangelical wing of the Church (of England) took the Articles at face value, this view has never been held by the whole Church. In 1643, (the same time America was being colonized), Archbishop John Bramhall boldly and publically argued against the royal decree. Out of this came the Oxford Movement of the 19th century which in many ways is still with us today in our First Amendment and its zeal against the government making any laws "respecting the establishment of religion or prohibiting the free exercise thereof." (See page 1 for more on this). It's still the attitude of our *Stew*

Westminster Confession of Faith (1645)

After the turbulent reign of Charles I of England, he was beheaded in 1643 and the English parliament commissioned the Westminster Confession of Faith. Puritan ministers met for 1,643 sessions and completed the Confession in 1649, although "those in power" claimed it was completed in 1645. Below is the Confession's statement of God which affected later Christian development:

I.

There is but one only living and true God, who is infinite in being and perfection, a most pure spirit, invisible, without body, parts, or passions, immutable, immense, eternal, incomprehensible, almighty, most wise, most holy, most free, most absolute, working all things according to the counsel of His own immutable and most righteous will, for His own glory; most loving, gracious, merciful, long suffering, abundant in goodness and truth, forgiving iniquity, transgression, and sin; the rewarder of them that diligently seek Him; and withal most just and terrible in His judgments, hating all sin, and who will by no means clear the guilty.

II.

God hath all life, glory, goodness, blessedness, in and of Himself; and is alone in and unto Himself all sufficient, not standing in need of any creatures which He hath made, nor deriving any glory from them, but only manifesting His own glory in, by, unto, and upon them; He alone is the fountain of all being, of whom, through whom, and to whom, are all things; and hath most sovereign dominion over them, to do by them, for them, and upon them whatsoever Himself pleaseth. In His sight all things are open and manifest; His knowledge is infinite, infallible, and contingent or upon the creature, so nothing is to Him contingent or uncertain. He is most holy in all His counsels, in all His works, and in all His commands. To Him is due from angles and men, and every other creature, whatsoever worship, service, or obedience He is pleased to require of them.

III.

In the unity of the Godhead there be three Persons of one substance, power, and eternity; God the Father, God the Son, and God the Holy Ghost. The Father is of none, neither begotten nor proceeding; the Son is eternally begotten of the Father; the Holy Ghost eternally proceeding from the Father and the Son

Index

About The Author

Dr. Stephenson has published several award-winning short stories in various magazines. Earned a B.S. in Behavioral Sciences; a M.A. in Literature (Both from University of Houston); and graduated Magma Cum Laude at Seminary with a Doctorate in Divinity. He is currently Director of Cherry Tree Ministries in Texas.